Love and birthday
good hopes
from
Marian and Hal

August 28, 1939

Note: The first oil well
was drilled in at
Titusville, Pa. on
August 28, 1850

Henry George

An Essay

BY MR. NOCK

JEFFERSON

◂

ON DOING THE RIGHT THING;
and other essays

◂

THE THEORY OF EDUCATION
IN THE UNITED STATES
(The Page-Barbour Lectures for 1930)

◂

(Edited, with Catherine Rose Wilson)
THE URQUHART-LE MOTTEUX
TRANSLATION OF THE WORKS
OF FRANCIS RABELAIS:
*With introduction, critical notes and
documentary illustrations*

◂

A JOURNAL OF THESE DAYS

◂

A JOURNEY INTO RABELAIS'S FRANCE

◂

OUR ENEMY, THE STATE

◂

FREE SPEECH AND PLAIN LANGUAGE

◂

HENRY GEORGE

Henry George

AN ESSAY BY

ALBERT JAY NOCK

WILLIAM MORROW & COMPANY

NEW YORK

HENRY GEORGE

COPYRIGHT - 1939
BY ALBERT JAY NOCK

All rights reserved. This book or parts thereof, may not be reproduced in any form without permission of the publisher.

PRINTED IN THE UNITED STATES OF AMERICA
BY QUINN & BODEN COMPANY, INC., RAHWAY, N. J.

PREFACE

TO EDWARD EPSTEAN

MY DEAR FRIEND: Eight years ago, when I was trifling with a literary project which you did not think was worth much, you told me rather brusquely that I had better drop it and do something with Henry George. Other friends made a similar suggestion afterwards; and I have accordingly written this little book for publication on the hundredth anniversary of George's birth. The credit of it, if there be any, would seem to belong to you by right of priority, so I cordially offer it to you, trusting that if it does not interest you on that account, you will still accept it as a reminder of my profound esteem and respect.

If the title leads you to expect a biography of George, you will be disappointed; my work is only a critical essay. I think that probably most of the significant incidents in his life come in for some sort of mention, but they are not developed beyond their bearing on the book's purpose. The official biography of George, written by his son, is still in print and easily available. In some respects it is one of the best works of its kind; in others, one of the worst. Its completeness, its superb accuracy, its apposite citations, its unfailing attention to the minutiæ of date, place and intimate circumstance, leave nothing to be desired; while its spirit is so devout as to make it almost more a memoir than a biography. On the other hand, the work is so poorly organized, so poorly edited, showing so little of the invaluable editorial sense of where an author should be content to rest lightly and where he should come down with his full weight, that it presents unnecessary difficulties to the reader. Its excellences are so far in excess of its defects, however, that it effectively discourages competition, especially on the part of one like myself, whose abilities run as little that way as his inclinations do, or even less.

No more should you expect to find here any exposition of George's philosophy. This can be got in the very best way at first hand from George's own works. Moreover, Mr. G. R. Geiger has lately published an excellent exposition of it in a volume which is also a guide to the whole literature of the subject. Nothing of the sort is within the scope of this essay. You will notice that I have carried exclusiveness so far as occasionally to use technical economic terms and phrases without pausing to define or explain them, even in a footnote. I have also once or twice criticized by bare statement some matter which might seem to demand that I should show cause; as, for instance, where I criticize George's proposals for a national confiscation of rent. If one were ever so little intent on converting one's readers, or prepossessing them towards George's economic doctrine, one would perhaps not do this; but this essay has no such ulterior motive.

My purpose is the humbler one of trying to answer certain questions concerning George and his career, which have never been satisfactorily answered; questions which seem not only striking enough to pique disinterested curiosity, but also important enough, especially in their implications, to make a competent answer desirable. Here you have a man who is one of the first half-dozen of the world's creative geniuses in social philosophy. The professor of philosophy in Columbia University puts it with simple truth of fact that "it would require less than the fingers of the two hands to enumerate those who, from Plato down, rank with Henry George among the world's social philosophers." Yet in this capacity he is today pre-eminently the Forgotten Man of Anglo-American civilization; he is almost wholly unknown, unremembered, save as a minor figure, more or less eccentric, in the public life of the last century.

How does this come about? I think it is without precedent. Holland remembers Spinoza for something more than his notoriety as an excommunicate Jew who in 1656 was troubling the Portuguese synagogue in Amsterdam. But Holland is Holland, one might say. Yes, but even in taking account of a society essentially barbarous, one would hardly go so far as to ascribe George's fate to natural causes alone—does not this same America today remember Emerson for something more than his associations with vegetarians and the communism of Brook Farm? Does not England remember Bentham for something more than his bizarre notions about the architecture of factories and prisons? George antagonized vested interests which were extremely powerful and influential—no doubt he did, but could any vested interests be *that* powerful? One must doubt it.

This essay, then, is nothing more than a review of George's career, in an attempt to lay a finger on the causes, both original and contributory, of an interesting social phenomenon. I hope you will find it reasonably successful, and in that hope I remain always, my dear friend, most affectionately yours,

ALBERT JAY NOCK.

Canaan, Conn.,
13 March, 1939.

1

HENRY GEORGE was born in the city of Philadelphia on the second day of September, 1839. By that time Philadelphia had succeeded in staggering out from under the weight of its prestige as the erstwhile national capital, and had settled back into the workaday routine of an industrial and mercantile town. It seems to have been America's nearest approach to a model city, for visiting foreigners, even captious Britons who landed with their tongues in their cheeks and chips on their shoulders, spoke well of it. Michel Chevalier, the eminent French economist and Saint-Simonian, by far the most competent observer who ever visited our shores, said it was "perhaps the most enlightened and refined city in the United States." As a rule, foreigners were mostly impressed by its external good order, its quietness, and the general air of austerity pervading its social life. Some bore witness to its minor amenities; for instance, the British consul T. C. Grattan, who arrived in 1839, left record of

Philadelphia as the only place in America where he could find fresh butter. Dickens, who came three years later, was less praiseful than the rest. He was frankly bored by Philadelphia's checkerboard layout and the straightness of the streets, all of which he seems to have ascribed to Quaker influence, for he says that when he walked about the town he felt he should be wearing Quaker garb and a broadbrimmed hat. Apparently he found little in Philadelphia that really interested him, except the practice of hiving up malefactors in solitary confinement. He regarded this as barbarous, and sermonized against it with all the vigour of his youthful pulpiteering; he was then thirty years old, and the adventures of Mr. Pickwick in the Fleet had already brought him before the English-speaking public as a mighty propagandist for prison reform.

The Englishry who came to look the city over were of the middle class, which had by that time begun to set the tone of British political and social life; and Philadelphia being one of the most Pecksniffian of American cities, they took its drabness and dulness as necessarily incidental to a properly regulated society; while for the same reason, on the other hand, its

An Essay

angular moralities and pretentious proprieties matched their own and were congenial to them. In the domesticity of Philadelphia they caught the distinct reflection of the precisianism which so distressed little Copperfield; in its schools they rubbed elbows with the guiding genius of Mr. Creakle, and found themselves at once in the familiar atmosphere of Salem House, with its strange unwholesome smell like "sweet apples wanting air, and rotten books." In Philadelphia's dominant views of life and demands on life they recognized those of Mr. Murdstone by the more serious side, and by the lighter side those of Mr. Quinion: the great figure of Poor Richard himself must have appeared to their eyes as a sort of improved and glorified Murdstone.

Hence not unnaturally the British middle-class spirit felt itself more at home in Philadelphia than in New York or Boston; much more than in the Southern and mid-Western cities. Philadelphia also strongly recommended itself to them by its dominant type of churchmanship, which was an evangelical Protestantism so uncompromising, so truculent and so aggressive as to seem well-nigh made to order on specifications drawn up by British Nonconformity.

It was the type prevailing in the North of Ireland, in Scotland, and in Britain's northern colonies; the type characterized by Edmund Burke as "the dissidence of Dissent, and the protestantism of the Protestant religion." Between this and the severe forthrightness of Quakerism on the one hand, and that of Low Church Episcopalianism on the other, there was a fair *modus vivendi* based on mutual respect, if on no more formal ground of agreement; and in their virulent antipathy to the Scarlet Woman on the Seven Hills they found at least one common motive of endeavour.

The servigerous Mrs. Trollope, mother of the great novelist, despite her dislike of almost everything American, looked on the civilization of Philadelphia with Miss Jane Murdstone's eyes, and found it not wholly objectionable. She managed to draw up a fairly restrained and accurate description of a specimen day in the domestic life of what she called "a Philadelphia lady of the first class." The picture is instructive chiefly—in fact, wholly—not for what it portrays, but for what it suggests without portrayal; that is to say, for its exhibit of the precise and horrifying correspondence of Philadelphia's representative social life with that of the sound Brit-

An Essay

ish Philistinism of Birmingham and Manchester. In her main interests, the Philadelphia lady is Mrs. Jellyby, with all Mrs. Jellyby's sincerity —for Mrs. Jellyby was sincere in her efforts to spread the Light upon those who sat in the darkness of Borrioboolagha—but without Mrs. Jellyby's dishevelment; that is to say, without her poverty. Dickens, like the good artist he was, knew he must make Mrs. Jellyby poor, for if she had been well-to-do she could hardly have served his purpose as a horrible example of draggle-tailed pietism. The Philadelphia lady's day is the day of a well-to-do British Philistiness; a day of tea-meetings, lectures, conscientious but more or less perfunctory superintendence of her household, attending the Dorcas Society, and hearing missionaries speak. While the ladies of the Dorcas Society are sewing for the heathen, Mrs. Trollope says:

Their talk is of priests and of missions; of the profits of their last sale, of their hopes from the next; of the doubt whether young Mr. This or young Mr. That should receive the fruits of it to fit him out for Liberia; of the very ugly bonnet seen at church on Sabbath morning, of the very handsome preacher who performed on Sabbath afternoon, and of the very large collection made on Sabbath evening.

So far Mrs. Trollope speaks with no undue exaggeration, and with a reasonable respect for the lady and for her occupations, however misguided and ineffectual they might appear, for lady and occupations alike are essentially those of the British Nonconformist middle class. She then goes on to say that after some hours with the Dorcas Society, the lady goes home, looks over the preparations for dinner, and sits down in the parlour to await her husband.

He comes, shakes hands with her, spits, and dines. The conversation is not much, and ten minutes suffices for the dinner; fruit and toddy, the newspaper and the workbag succeed. In the evening the gentleman, being a savant, goes to the Wister Society, and afterwards plays a snug rubber at a neighbour's. The lady receives at tea a young missionary and three members of the Dorcas Society; and so ends her day.

What a day! one says at once. What an existence! The husband has somewhat the air of having been lugged in by the ears as an embellishment; yet as one recalls the figure of Mr. Gradgrind, "a kind of cannon loaded to the

An Essay 15

muzzle with facts," one thinks that here too, probably, Mrs. Trollope may have exaggerated but little, and that the parallel with the sound British middle-class ideal of domesticity still holds. Mr. Gradgrind, Mr. Plugson of Undershot, Mr. Dombey, Mr. Bottles, in all likelihood would not have spit, for tobacco-chewing never took any great hold on England; but in other respects any of them might have sat for the sketch of the Philadelphia lady's husband. The thing to be observed, however, is that in her "portrait of a lady" Mrs. Trollope lays her finger on the one characteristic mark of American social life which impresses a civilized observer as most appalling, and does it as unconsciously, or at most half-consciously, as her gifted son brings out the identical mark of social life in Barchester—its overpowering dulness, its hideousness, its consummate ennui.

II

The same mark is quite as unconsciously brought out in the youthful correspondence of Henry George, and in a sort of diary which he kept for a short time at the age of fourteen or so. The chief value of these documents is in their testimony to the kind of civilization that Murdstone and Quinion had built up, and the institutions which they had devised to promote and exalt the ideals of that civilization and effectively to discourage any other; above all, effectively to suffocate such possible wayward hankerings after any other as the youthful Philadelphian, in his boredom, might sometimes feel. These institutions were founded on Murdstone's great dictum that "to the young this is a world for action; not for moping and droning in," the dictum so capably sugar-coated by Longfellow, who might quite reasonably take title as Mr. Murdstone's American poet-laureate by brevet. The purpose of political institutions was to help business; the Constitutional Convention of 1787, under Murdstone's personal direction, had settled that very commendably. On full-dress occasions, say, once a year on Independence Day, Murdstone was willing to listen to the archaic doctrine of the Declaration of Independence, that "to secure these rights governments are instituted among men," but he did it in the same spirit of vacuous formalism with which on Sundays he listened to the outpourings of the Rev. Josiah Jupp on some point of theological paradox. He likewise made

An Essay 17

no great difficulties about the proposal to tack on a Bill of Rights to the tail-end of the Constitution, but again he did so on the understanding, more or less explicit, that in any exigent circumstances it should not "count"; and the Judiciary Act of 1789 would see to that. The logic of his position was simple and rigorous. Whatever is good for business is good for society, and government is instituted for the good of society; therefore the government should help business. It is rather a rough-and-ready type of syllogism, perhaps, and one might cavil a little at its major premise; but Mr. Murdstone was a practical man and had no patience with logic-chopping.

The basic principle of human conduct which animated Mr. Murdstone's civilization was well formulated for Henry George's benefit by an anonymous person whom George described thirty years later as "a gentleman who wanted me to go into business as a boy in a store." George says, "I had nothing, no particular facility, yet I remember his saying to me, 'If you are honest, if you are steady, if you are industrious, you can certainly look forward to being able to retire at forty with comfort for the rest of your days.' " This fine precept, with its sure forecast of reward, might be called Mr. Murdstone's Golden Rule. It brings to mind once more the forlorn figure of Poor Richard as he entered Philadelphia afoot, friendless and resourceless, with—what was it?—one forgets; was it a loaf of bread under one arm and a shirt wrapped up in brown paper under the other, and his clothes out at elbows?—something of the sort, anyway. Yet as he went on diligently striving by the light of Mr. Murdstone's Golden Rule, see what he became; see with what orderly steps he kept moving from one pitch of distinction and usefulness to a higher, until Europe and America came finally to know and praise him as the typical American, the official American exponent, one might say, of the Murdstonian philosophy of life.

With such an example before its eyes, Philadelphia provided opportunities for its young men to go on perfecting themselves in this philosophy after they had passed through their preparatory course of Salem House and Mr. Creakle. These opportunities were chiefly vocational, as was to be expected; they contemplated the material and practical, from the point of view of one who wishes to get on in the world; indeed, from the days of Rittenhouse

An Essay

and Rush, Philadelphia has always been strong for turning the natural sciences to practical account. The Franklin Institute, for instance, which maintained lectureships giving a semi-popular treatment of such subjects—and perhaps still does—was incorporated in 1824 "for the promotion and encouragement of manufactures and the mechanic and useful arts," and the general run of such enterprises tended in that direction. On the other hand, opportunities for progress in the liberal arts, in the study of literature, philosophy and history, for example, were harder for a youth to come by. The discipline of Salem House and Mr. Creakle had not prepared him for anything of the kind, and what impulse he had towards it must needs be largely self-sprung; moreover, the Murdstonian philosophy made but little place in human life for any such pursuit and was inclined to disparage it as tending to take one's mind off the really serious purposes of existence. Hence if a lad turned to reading, he did it on his own, taking more or less indiscriminately what he could get, with no very clear purpose to guide him. His choice of reading, too, was arbitrarily limited, for the Rev. Josiah Jupp, in collusion with Murdstone, had set up an *index expur-*

gatorius as stringent as the Vatican's, and far less liberal. Religious books, provided they were sound in the Protestant faith and Protestant ethics, were free to young and old alike; even religious romance and poetry were free. So were scientific works, save such as might breed doubt of the Mosaic cosmogony, the Biblical miracles, special creation, the Noachian deluge, the episode of Babel, and Archbishop Ussher's chronology. So were many books of travel, especially those which dealt with the work of scientific expeditions, the experience of missionaries, and researches in the Holy Land. A carefully bowdlerized version of Franklin's *Autobiography,* and innumerable vulgarizations of the Murdstonian philosophy which were essentially like it, were of course regarded as the ideal guide of youth. Secular works which dealt with the romance, poetry and beauty of life, however, were pretty strictly kept away from youthful eyes. For this reason the type of reading most likely to interest the young had to be got at surreptitiously, when got at at all. Henry George left record that even the innocuous *Scottish Chiefs* was disallowed, and he had to do his reading of it on the sly; and that when he went to sea at the age of sixteen, for a voyage

An Essay

of eleven months as a foremast-boy, the stock of literature furnished him by his family consisted of a Bible and a copy of *James's Anxious Inquirer*.

Dramatic literature lay under the general obloquy resting upon stage-plays as a heritage from the times when actors were officially listed as rogues and vagabonds. Even Shakespeare was gone at with long teeth. The man who so aroused the wrath of Mrs. Trollope by asserting that "Shakespeare, madame, is obscene; and, thank God, we are sufficiently advanced to have found it out," was not a Philadelphian—he hailed from Cincinnati—but he was unmistakably in Philadelphia's best tradition. Most of us who as yet have both our feet well outside the grave can remember the expurgated editions of Shakespeare got up for the use of the young; perhaps they still exist. George says that in his boyhood there were several theatres in Philadelphia—in fact, the Walnut Street Theatre is supposed to be the oldest in the country; it was built in 1808—but they were patronized only by the scandalous and ungodly. In this connexion he tells a story which illustrates a curious and naïve tenet of the Murdstonian philosophy; which is, that you can change the character of a thing by changing its name. Observers have often remarked that belief in this miracle, giving, as it does, to Anglo-American institutions their peculiar character of slipperiness and obliquity, must be put down as the first article of Anglo-American faith. George says that an enterprising man named Barnum went to Philadelphia, and saw that if he could set up a theatre that the godly would go to, it would pay extremely well. So he set up one, but he did not call it a theatre. He called it a lecture-room, and in that lecture-room he gave theatrical representations, six nights a week and two matinees, to crowded houses.

III

Thus when all comes to all, one is well prepared to find that the available records of George's boyhood reveal an extremely straitened intellectual and cultural and social existence. His diary discloses no serious activity more interesting or improving than a pretty steady attendance on Sunday-school, church, the Franklin Institute lectures, and seeing a "panorama of Europe." George seems, perhaps naturally, to have been for most of his time in

An Essay

a state of very imperfect correspondence with his environment. He had but little schooling; Salem House and Mr. Creakle were quite too much for him, apparently. He tried his hand at the primary and grammar grades in four different schools, but did little in any, and finally reaching the secondary grade, he did no better; he gave up at the end of five months, with the record, as he himself put it in later life, of having been "for the most part idle, and wasted time." He never tried again; this was the end of his formal education.

A contemporary recalls George "going to church every Sunday, walking between his two older sisters, followed by his father and mother; all of them so neat, trim and reserved." The picture rather reminds one of David Copperfield's account of "the tremendous visages with which we used to go to church"; Mr. and Miss Murdstone and David's mother in decorous procession, with David disconsolately bringing up the rear. Yet of all the influences which were brought to bear upon George's early education, strange to say, the most valuable and most fruitful in its indirect effects was the one that was exercised at large by the Rev. Josiah Jupp. What with the allopathic dosage of church,

Sunday-school and family prayer, morning and evening, a child got some considerable acquaintance with the King James Version and the Book of Common Prayer; that is to say, some acquaintance with the very best English usage. Even the most inattentive and refractory child could hardly hope to escape this; and a child who was moderately intelligent and biddable was unconsciously in a way to let the acquaintance run on into a profitable familiarity. By this indirect method of pure hearsay, George learned to use the English language as it should be used. When he was forty years old, he came suddenly before the English-speaking world as the possessor of a superb English prose style, a distinguished master of English idiom, and there is no way to account for this proficiency save by reference to that one invaluable experience of his childhood. One of George's expositors has cited certain letters written to his sister from California when he was in his twentieth year, as "giving some idea of the crudeness of his own writing at the time." One hardly knows what to say to this. Of course one may not be sure that this critic's standards of style are the ones generally accepted, but if they are the same, or anywhere near the same, his choice

An Essay   25

of examples is most unfortunate. Here, for instance, is a line or two from the first one which he chooses to illustrate his point:

> What a time we live in, when great events follow one another so quickly that we have not space for wonder! We are driving at a killing pace somewhere—Emerson says to heaven, and Carlyle says to the other place, but however much they differ, go we surely do.

If this be crude writing, one can only say that there is a bad outlook ahead for the swift, straightforward, correct, forceful monosyllabic idiom of New Testament narrative, which we who were brought up in the times of ignorance were fain to regard as pretty good. *A certain man had two sons: and the younger of them said to his father, Father, give me the portion of goods that falleth to me; and he divided unto them his living.* In fact, one can hardly help thinking that this critic might have done well to apply the yardstick of New Testament narrative to the kind of English that George wrote at the age of twenty, or indeed at seventeen, and then apply it to the kind of English that he himself writes. Here, for example, is a bit of narrative written by George at seventeen, on shipboard, which even R. H. Dana might have found quite acceptable, one thinks, in point of style:

The wind, which had been strong from aft the day before, during the middle watch died away, and was succeeded by a calm until 8 A.M., when a stiff breeze from the south sprang up, accompanied by showers of rain. At 12 M. all hands were called to reef. While reefing the foretopsail, the parrel of the yard gave way, causing a great deal of trouble, and keeping all hands from dinner. . . . The rest of the day was rainy, with wind constantly varying, keeping us hauling on the braces. Thus closed the most miserable Fourth of July that I have ever yet spent.

But however crude or however finished George's early style may be adjudged by what Aristotle calls "the determination of the judicious," its correspondence with his later style is reasonably evident. Both his early and later styles, moreover, carry unmistakably the suggestion of being based on a pretty sound acquaintance with the idiom of the Authorized Version and the Book of Common Prayer—the suggestion which a person of even a moderate literary experience can always detect in the work of any writer who has undergone that salutary discipline. Moreover, and finally, there is no known source from which George could have derived his style, be it early or late, crude or finished, good or bad, except the kind of English that prevailed around him in his early years in Philadelphia. Murdstone must be given credit, it seems, for having no prejudice against classical idiomatic English; in fact, it is clear that he and the Rev. Josiah Jupp conspired, perhaps unconsciously, to institutionalize classical English and invest it with very powerful recommendations. Its force, rhythm and cadence were intimately associated with the expression of religious hopes, beliefs and aspirations; it was the spiritual vernacular. Its use marked the way of temporary escape sought by uncounted thousands whom the tedium and hideousness of the Murdstonian civilization had oppressed beyond unaided endurance, and over whose heads the sky was of iron and brass. The régime of Murdstone had little enough to give Henry George, but this one great though unconsidered gift it gave him; it gave him a competent use of his native language in all its purity, its abounding richness and its imposing nobleness.

The lighter side of life in the Murdstonian

civilization, what there was of it, was directed and regulated by Murdstone's factotum, Mr. Quinion. Murdstone did not concern himself with it, save to restrict and limit it wherever he could, and afterwards think no more about it. Within the limits thus set by the demands of life's serious side, Quinion's policy was the liberal one of letting the youthful spirit entertain itself by whatever means it might be able to turn up. These means were perforce few and simple, and up to the period of adolescence, at any rate, they were fairly reputable. George's diary mentions skating, sleigh-riding with an uncle, building a toy ship, hobnobbing with relatives and with one or two of his sisters' girl-cronies. A contemporary says that the wharves were a favourite ground for gang-play; and a letter from George's mother written after he had departed on a second long sea-voyage, shows that mixed parties of boys and girls amused themselves with parlour-games and kissing forfeits. She wrote:

You have just passed your nineteenth birthday. Did you think of it, or were you too busy? If you had been home we would have had a jollification. What a kissing-time there would have been, play-

An Essay

ing Copenhagen, and so forth. Hen, kissing is quite out of fashion since you left; no kissing-parties at all, I believe.

At nineteen, or even considerably earlier, the youthful spirit was indeed pretty well graduated out of kissing-parties and had gone in for an order of diversions winked at by Mr. Quinion as more consistent with maturity, and not to be too strictly reprehended, provided they were judiciously indulged in. One might perhaps put it more frankly that they were the only diversions which Quinion understood; his conception of life's resources on the lighter side was as narrow as Murdstone's conception of its resources on the more serious side. We all remember Mr. Quinion's rough joviality, his badinage, his end-to-end consumption of cigars, and the aura of beer and gin that always hung about him; and we meet his spirit at once in a letter which one of George's companions wrote in 1863, reminiscent of their early days together as members of the "Lawrence Literary Society."

Can you or I forget the gay, refreshing and kindred spirits that formed that association . . . its sympathy with ghost-stories, boxing-gloves, fencing-foils and deviltry . . . its test of merit and standard of membership, to drink red-eye, sing good songs and smoke lots of cigars.

George's own diary, in his eighteenth year, describes an evening spent in exercises quite to Quinion's taste; a round of cigar-shops and gin-mills with one pal and another; punch-drinking and impromptu speech-making; staging a boxing-match on a street-corner; and a return home "about daybreak." In 1858, too, after George had gone to seek his fortune in California, one of his friends wrote him regretfully:

I would have given anything to have you there this evening, my dear fellow, for we are going to kick hell up again tonight. We have got plenty of the very best imported brandy and port wine, for we have a first-rate fellow in our room who is in a wholesale drug house on Market Street, and he brings all the liquors home with him, so that they don't cost us anything, and his employers are very willing that he should have them in his room for the purpose, as they suppose, of trying experiments, though they little imagine what kind of experiments they are used for.

While it is true that no one in George's early entourage discerned in him the promise of one of the few really first-class minds of his time, or

An Essay 31

of any time, the fact is not remarkable, for at that stage of development such a promise is seldom clear enough, even under the most favourable circumstances, to be easily discerned. The thing to be remarked is that if it had been discerned, no one knew what to do about it. The discipline of Salem House and Mr. Creakle, while perhaps excellent in its way, was not designed to meet the requirements of a first-class mind. The Murdstonian civilization could do nothing with a first-class mind save to train it in some way leading to the service of the Murdstonian philosophy; perhaps in the law, in the church, in medicine, but of course by all means preferably, in business. In the nature of things, Murdstone could not contemplate any kind of training that from the beginning was not narrowly vocational, because "to the young this is a world for action, not for moping and droning in"; and the formative exercises appropriate to a first-class mind which has no turn at all for action but only a pronounced turn for thinking, are wholly inconsistent with that view of the world; and since Murdstone held to that view and would admit no other, he was unable to devise such exercises or to apply them.

Thus Henry George grew up to manhood

knowing no language or literature but his own, and his own only at haphazard; knowing human history only by what little of it he could pick up from variously qualified sources. He had none of the well-rounded cultural experience which bears in due measure and proportion upon all five of humanity's fundamental instincts; the instinct of expansion, the instinct of intellect and knowledge, of religion and morals, of beauty and poetry, of social life and manners. A contemporary remarked that George's mind "was a flower of slow growth; at thirty-seven he was just reaching mental manhood." In some respects, indeed, he never reached it, and obviously could not have reached it even measurably at a normal age, because the cultural experience which his type of mind required was wholly lacking. His cultural environment was the civilization of Murdstone and Quinion; it was marked by a monstrously over-developed sense of expansion, a defective sense of intellect, a defective sense of religion and morals, a stunted sense of beauty, a stunted sense of social life and manners; and for a mind eminently philosophical, the continuous experience of such an environment is to the last degree debilitating and retarding.

2

LOOKING over the whole length and breadth of America, then, one saw in the civilization of Philadelphia about the best that Murdstone and Quinion could do. Society there had gone about as far in the way of humanizing itself as the Murdstonian philosophy of life could carry it. Most parts of America, virtually all of it, reflected Murdstone and Quinion at their worst. Murdstone had never gone into Aristotle's doctrine of excess and defect, or considered what he says about virtue residing in a mean; hence practically the whole of American society expressed the Murdstonian philosophy run out into disorder and degeneration through fantastic excess. Whether at its best in Philadelphia, however, or at its worst elsewhere, the civilization of all America was the authentic unalloyed civilization of Murdstone and Quinion; the country knew no other.

While George remained at home he had the advantage, whatever it amounted to, of rubbing elbows with the best that this civilization was producing, and of profiting, as much as might be, from the impact of its influence during his formative years. Leaving home at the age of sixteen as no better than a wanderer, little better than one of Mr. Murdstone's "workhouse casuals," he met that civilization at its worst and meanest, and saw little of any other phase of it throughout his career. His sojourns in other lands, confined as they were to English-speaking countries, brought him no change of spiritual and cultural environment. Towards the end of his life he and his wife made one rapid tour through Italy, where he wrote a friend that "you would get sick of old masters"; then through Switzerland and France, but only as sight-seers, flitting about at pure hazard, and having, as he said, "a good time in our own way, unknown and unknowing, and working our way by signs, largely," after the approved fashion of the American tourist. Of the actual civilization of the Continent, which was at its very best in his lifetime, he saw nothing and knew nothing. After Philadelphia, his sphere of social experience was limited to California, New York, England, Ireland, New Zealand, Australia; and there, wherever he went, the civilization surrounding him was none other than the old familiar civilization of Murdstone and Quinion, and he saw it regularly by its worst side.

One wonders what the balance of gain and loss might have been if this condition had been even ever so little different. The question is an idle one, of course, but the chief interest in a study of George's career is that at every tack and turn one is forced to keep asking it. What might have been the course of his life if, say, he had stuck to his schooling, taken advantage of such cultural opportunities as Philadelphia offered—there were some—and at seventeen, like Mr. Jefferson at the same age, had edged his way into the society of experienced and accomplished men who were resolutely alien to the prevailing civilization? Such alien spirits exist everywhere; there were three even in "Devilsburg," as in his student days Mr. Jefferson used to style the seat of William and Mary College. Philadelphia of the 'fifties and 'sixties had some who were so eminent that Murdstone and his retainers were forced to give them a grudging and perfunctory recognition. Like Fauquier, Small and Wythe at Williamsburg, such men would have been quick to see in Henry George the latent abilities which were quite beyond the reach of Mr. Creakle's apprehension, and it would be in the nature of things that association with them should mature those abilities and give the best direction to their development; a direction, at all events, which they never had. A like association did just that for Mr. Jefferson, whose abilities were largely of the same order, and whose natural endowment seems to have been no greater than George's, save for the unweariable iron physique which George never had—he died of premature old age, culminating in a stroke of apoplexy when he was fifty-eight years old.

But, to repeat, all speculation on this point is idle, because an insuperable barrier stood in George's way; the barrier of great poverty. Mr. Jefferson came of a rich family; Henry George's family was extremely, even miserably, poor. This is not by any means to say that in the Philadelphia of that day a very poor boy might not manage to go to school, or that poverty would of itself be any bar to association with cultivated people; but the obligations which poverty forced on George made anything of the kind virtually impossible. He was the oldest son in a family of ten children, and the family's income came to sixty-six dollars per year, per head.

One of the interesting peculiarities of Murdstone's civilization was that it gave involuntary poverty the status of an institution. Poverty existed by divine right, like monarchy in earlier times. Preaching on the text, *The poor ye have always with you,* the Rev. Josiah Jupp argued that we must and should always have them with us, because such is God's will. Hence it did not occur to Murdstone, sitting in his pew, to question the status of poverty or to wonder whether, as a whole, the society which he was organizing and directing would not get on better if so many of its members were not so desperately poor. Charity towards the poor was a religious duty, and right well did Murdstone and his compeers in Philadelphia fulfil it, according to their lights; but any radical interference with the incidence of poverty, any but the most superficial inquiry into its causes, was presumptuous if not impious, and savoured a little of heresy. Those who, like Henry George, had the yoke of poverty laid on them at birth must bear it gladly; the spirit of rebellion, complaint or repining was wicked and against God. Archbishop Cranmer's divines had long ago laid down the law for them in the Church Catechism, on which they were bred from earliest childhood, that they should "do their duty in that station of life unto which it had pleased God to call them"; and that was that.

So, for a child in Henry George's position, the thing was to get out into the activities of Murdstone's world as soon as possible, and, as Cranmer's divines put it, to learn and labour truly to get his own living, and withal to succour his father and mother; in more modern phrase, to help out the family. This being so, he had little chance for any improving experience which was not pretty strictly practical and vocational. The discipline of Salem House was thought to be quite right for the purpose contemplated; any other discipline, or any extended experience bearing in another direction, might encourage a meditative child to regard the world as "a place for moping and droning in," which would never do. George had already undergone the discipline of Salem House with such indifferent results that anything further of the kind seemed inexpedient in any circumstances, let alone such as were pressing on him to get himself off his family's hands; so he began to look more or less vaguely about him for something to do.

However little he had profited by Mr. Creakle's régime, it seems to have had the effect of permanently fixing George's views of the nature and purpose of education. All his life he appears to have been pretty strictly a vocationalist. At the age of forty-one, facing the question whether to put his elder son into a newspaper-office or send him to Harvard College, he decided against Harvard, saying that if the lad went there, he would learn a great deal that he must afterwards spend time on unlearning; whereas "going to newspaper-work, you will come in touch with the practical world, will be getting a profession and learning to make yourself useful." At about the same time he wrote his younger son that he had "come to the conclusion that if you can find a place to set type, it will be best for you not to go back to school after Christmas. I don't like your leaving school until you have got further along, but you are getting so old now [the boy was sixteen] that it is important that you should learn to make a living for yourself, for that is by far the most important part of education." All this is precisely in the vein of Mr. Creakle; a great refinement indeed upon Mr. Creakle's truculence, but the principle is exactly that of Murdstone's practical man in education; it is the tap-root of Mr. Creakle's pedagogy.

Moreover, for the ineducable nine-tenths, or more, of the human race, this principle is a sound one. The trouble was by no means that the principle is unsound—quite the contrary—but only that Murdstone and Mr. Creakle claimed too much for it. They made it applicable to the whole of the human race instead of to the vast ineducable majority, and thereby their practical measures tended to leave the small but socially valuable minority somewhat out in the cold. It may be that George was quite right in the disposition he made of his children, but his sweeping statement that learning how to make a living is by far the most important part of education seems to show that it had not occurred to him to differentiate between the needs of the ineducable mass and those of the educable few; and the ground of this failure in discrimination runs straight back to the régime of Mr. Creakle.

This failure begot another, equally serious, the failure to differentiate between education and training. George never perceived that Mr.

An Essay

Creakle's system, excellent, useful and largely appropriate as it may have been, was not an educational system, though everyone agreed to call it such and believed it to be such. It had nothing to do with education; it was a system of training, perfectly suited in principle to the needs and capacities of the ineducable masses, but as perfectly unsuited to those of the educable few. Hence when George defined "the most important part of education" in rigidly vocational terms, he was unconsciously subscribing to an egregious error.

This could not well be otherwise, for George had never been in circumstances which permitted him to suspect this error, let alone perceive it. Murdstone did not differentiate education from training; if he had interrupted his preoccupations by thinking about the matter at all, he would have thought they were the same thing. Quinion would have been amused by the suggestion that they are not the same thing, and would have asked what of it. Mr. Creakle, glowering in his arm-chair, with his prodigious watch-chain and seals, his cane, his buttered toast, his apoplectic visage, his starting veins, gave forth the doctrine that they are and ever were and ever must be the same thing. What then was Henry George to think? All over the wide expanse of the Murdstonian civilization in both hemispheres were springing up innumerable institutions, calling themselves educational, which in principle were replicas of Salem House and were administered by old pupils of Mr. Creakle, thoroughly imbued with Mr. Creakle's doctrine; and as we have seen, the Murdstonian civilization is the only one that George ever knew.

At the time when George's sons were born, Ernest Renan was formulating this terrible sentence:

> Les pays qui, comme les États-Unis, ont créé un enseignement populaire considérable sans instruction supérieure sérieuse, expieront longtemps encore leur faute par leur médiocrité intellectuelle, leur grossièreté de mœurs, leur esprit superficiel, leur manque d'intelligence générale.

A civilization which, through its foremost exponent, accounts for itself in such terms as these, remained always unknown to George. It is an interesting fact that even in his later years when more doors were open to him, his choice of associates tended regularly towards men who were intellectually self-made. This choice was

An Essay 43

apparently deliberate. His biographer says of his friends and counselors in San Francisco, while he was writing his first work on economics, that "not one of them had received a finished education, in the European sense. All were positive, aggressive, independent men, representing distinct opinions, tastes and habits of life. Each had made his way in the community chiefly by the force of his own nature." Throughout his career Henry George remained one of the gentlest, most sympathetic, most affable and least ostentatious of men, but all his actual intimacies were with what we loosely call "men of the people" whose cultural attainments were very limited. His distaste for the typical academic mind was not without reason; it is understandable. He saw the country's institutional life in bondage to the Murdstonian system of ethics, economics and politics; he saw instruction on these subjects thoroughly committed to what someone has wittily called "the hire learning"; and it seemed to him that this tainted the character, not only of all America's academic pursuits, but also of those who would consent to engage in them. He apparently was persuaded that side by side with a perverted system of instruction in ethics, economics and politics, no instruction on any subject could be respectable. When still a young man, in a lecture before the University of California, he spoke of the "pretentious quackery" surrounding the study of economics, and bore down with great severity upon "the men, and unfortunately they are plenty, who pass through the whole educational machinery, and come out but learned fools, . . . all the more pitiable, all the more contemptible, all the more in the way of real progress, because they pass, with themselves and others, as educated men."

All he said in this strain is very just; but again one must discriminate. It would appear at least possible that George's justifiable dislike and distrust of the typical academic mind spread out into something like a passive general aversion from a cultivated society. Perhaps the circumstances of his career made this inevitable —one cannot say with any certainty—but on the face of it the thing seems unfortunate, for it kept him in habitual association with persons whose range of knowledge, intellectual discipline and cultural attainments were in no way superior to his own; for the most part, indeed, inferior. Thus his experience of men, large as it was, was limited; it was abundant, but not

An Essay

varied; a great and profitable area of human association remained closed to him, apparently by his own choice. His economic doctrines latterly brought him into collision with some of the ablest men of the century, and in each instance he carried off a hollow controversial victory. One wonders what the result might have been if he had appeared before them, not in the repellent guise of a polemist, propagandist, popular orator and factional fugleman, but in all his natural amiability as a simple fellow-labourer, a fellow-citizen of the great republic of intellect and knowledge, a fellow-philosopher who had worked his way through to the end of a new and far-reaching line of social philosophy.

II

When George got out from under Mr. Creakle's hand at fourteen years of age, he picked up some odd jobs as an errand-boy, packer and minor clerk. After two years of this he went to sea as foremast-boy on a ramshackle old East Indiaman of 600 tons, called the *Hindoo,* for a voyage of fourteen months, touching at Melbourne and Calcutta; and on his return, at seventeen, his real search for an occupation began.

It began at a bad time. Murdstone had never been able to make the economic machinery of his system run evenly; it ran by fits and starts. Apparently there was no way to get it to run evenly. In 1839, the year of George's birth, it was not running at all; the country was at the bottom of the worst depression in its history. Andrew Jackson's fiscal policies had brought about a crash in 1837 which prostrated Murdstone's whole system, financial, industrial and commercial, subjecting it to ten years of most drastic liquidation. Philadelphia was hit especially hard, and the effects of the depression, particularly its moral effect, lasted a long time. Hence even as late as 1856 when another bad panic was about to break, "unemployment" showed a distinct prospect of becoming a permanent problem; wages were low, and work was hard to get.

George's family could not have helped him much at the best of times. His father, like many others, did not fit particularly well into Murdstone's scheme of things; to do so, one had to have a rather special faculty or aptitude, and George's father seems not to have had it. He

An Essay

was for a time a minor Federal jobholder, a clerk in the Philadelphia custom-house, and as everyone knows, jobholding does not attract persons capable of doing much else, nor is it calculated either to stimulate ambition or to sharpen initiative. He did, however, give it up in 1831, for a partnership in a small concern which published religious literature of the Protestant Episcopal persuasion, and did a considerable trade in Sunday-school books. He carried on this business for seventeen years, and then returned to a clerkship in the custom-house where he managed to weather through the changes and chances of political tenure for fourteen years. He lost his place in 1861, when he was sixty-four, and wrote his son Henry, who was then in California, that "I do not know to-night but that I shall be a pauper tomorrow. . . . If I am discharged, I know not what will become of us." After his dismissal, he appears to have contemplated a turn at the ship-brokerage business with another discharged employé of the custom-house, but there is no record of this enterprise. He lived another nineteen years, however, in good health and with his faculties unimpaired, dying in 1883 at the age of eighty-five; his wife survived him by one week.

He got a job in a printing-house for his son Henry in 1856, when the latter returned from the voyage to India on the *Hindoo*. Henry stuck at it for seven months and then quit it, dissatisfied; his pay was two dollars a week, and his foreman was tyrannous. His father then got him a chance with another printing-concern which latterly published a notable denominational weekly, the *Episcopal Register,* an organ of the militant Low Church Episcopalian element in the northern states. They made hard terms with Henry, offering him what amounted to a bound apprenticeship of four years with pay starting at $2.25 a week; he did not take the job. Labour was in a buyer's market with a vengeance, at that period. Henry could turn up nothing permanent, nothing which held any prospect of a future; nor could his father's influence as a vestryman of St. Paul's parish turn up anything for him that was worth having. During his eighteenth year, however, he got enough experience at odd jobs to round him off as a first-class journeyman compositor and a very fair practical printer. He was already near enough an able seaman to be called one; he could "handle, reef and steer"; in fact, when in that year he shipped on a topsail schooner to try his luck in Boston, the captain paid him off at the full rate of an able seaman, saying he had fully earned it. Thus with two trades at his command, good trades, useful trades and normally not overcrowded, he could find no chance to exercise either of them on terms which would assure him anything even approaching a hand-to-mouth existence.

George was a depression-baby; industrial depression put its mark on him at birth as deeply and indelibly as war puts its mark on a war-baby. As a boy he saw depression and the effects of depression all about him at home, and when the *Hindoo* made her first port at Melbourne, in far-off Australia, there also he saw depression and the effects of depression; he wrote that times were said to be "very hard ashore, thousands with nothing to do, and nothing to eat." On his return home he saw and heard of little else; the subject had taken complete possession of the public mind. One of his juvenile chums even wrote a ramshackle essay on the depression for the "Lawrence Literary Society." He found things no better in Boston; he could get nothing there; and when he came back to Philadelphia from his unsuccessful errand in Boston, he found that conditions had worsened even in the short time he was away. "The times here are very hard," he wrote a friend, "and are getting worse and worse every day, factory after factory suspending, and discharging its hands. There are thousands of hard-working mechanics now out of employment in this city." The lure of gold drew his attention to the west coast, where miners were reported to be taking great fortunes out of the earth with little effort. The great gold-rush to California was over, and one's chances were no doubt not so good as they had been; still, one must go somewhere, and chances looked no better anywhere else that one could hear of. He determined to go, and his only means of going was by working his way. "There is a ship loading here for San Francisco," he wrote, "on board of which I have been promised a berth, but in the present stagnation of business it is doubtful whether she will get off before a month or two, at least." Again the depression! After a good deal of effort, however, he got a place as storekeeper on the lighthouse-tender *Shubrick,* a side-wheeler of some 400 tons, which was fitting out for duty on the Pacific coast; and reaching the coast meant a five-months voyage from the Philadelphia navy-yard by way of the Straits of Magellan. He sailed late in December, 1857; he was then in his eighteenth year.

III

Meanwhile Murdstone had been getting rich by leaps and bounds. Depressions are always a great harvest-time for strong, astute and unscrupulous men, and Murdstone was clawing money with both hands out of the long depression-period into which George was born, and throughout which George's youth was spent. His success had come in for unfavourable notice; there was a strong general impression that Murdstone was overdoing the thing a little, and that some sort of check should be put on his activities. This impression ran back to the time of Jackson's great war on the Bank of the United States, which was the immediate precursor of the depression. Before that time, in a social sense, America was fairly well undifferentiated. Some men were richer than others, but colossal fortunes had not yet appeared, and the rich were unostentatious. Murdstone lived in reasonable simplicity, largely by preference, but largely also in conformity to the rough and superficial spirit of equality which then prevailed—the spirit expressed in the saying that "in America, one man is just as good as another, or a little better." Jackson's administration paraded the raw-head-and-bloody-bones of "the money power," and spread the fear of it throughout the land. Jackson went out of office in 1836, having destroyed the Bank of the United States; the crash came in 1837, just as his successor took over. The long period of appalling liquidation followed, and was protracted by a violent secondary crash in 1842 and a panic in 1857.

Jackson did not conjure up the demon of "the money power" which he put on display; he found it ready to his hand. The Bank of the United States was in Philadelphia; and quite early in the century a small group of Philadelphians took fright at the impending menace of "the money power," and started a violent crusade against it; in fact, it was largely, perhaps chiefly, due to their efforts that the Bank's charter failed of renewal. Thus Henry George's boyhood was spent where a good deal of polemic talk about the money power was current; especially since the president of the defunct

Bank immediately started another one under a Pennsylvania state charter, and this bank failed in 1842, precipitating the crisis above referred to. True, growing children are inattentive to such matters; they have their own interests to look after. Still, impressions unheeded in childhood often make themselves felt in later life, almost always giving no clear sense of when or how they were originally formed. It seems most improbable that in the great centre of agitation over this subject the life of a child could go on in complete unawareness. It is ten to one that members of the Lawrence Literary Society, which was formed for the study of "poetry, economics and Mormonism," and had already listened to a youthful essay on the depression, heard talk now and then about the menace of the money power, and had mentioned it in meeting.

The Philadelphian crusaders against the money power campaigned in the name of democracy; they thought democracy was imperilled by the weight of Murdstone's bulging pockets. Democracy had but just got over being a term of reproach, and had taken on a certain specious respectability. Politicians no longer execrated the "turbulence," the "excesses," the "dangers" of democracy, as Hamilton, Madison, Morris, Gerry, Randolph, did so wholeheartedly in 1787. They sang another tune after 1828, for "the filthy democrats" were organized and had votes, and were to be flattered and gulled accordingly. Jackson had led a successful "revolt of the masses," and democracy was their watchword. It was not a descriptive term; it meant simply nothing, it had always meant nothing; originally a term of inane abuse, it had now become an abracadabra, a conjuring-term for the use of pettifoggers and demagogues in managing their herd. Its actual function was the disreputable one of disguising some special interest, for which the favour of the masses was to be gained. Accepting Dr. Johnson's sturdy definition of patriotism as the last refuge of a scoundrel, the next to the last has surely been democracy. Nevertheless, after Jackson's revolt, the word was bandied about from mouth to ear of honest people who gave it all sorts of fanciful meaning in their own minds, or else did not trouble themselves to care whether it had any meaning. George came to maturity in an environment of this illiterate and unconscious ignorance concerning democracy. The pæan of praise to democracy saluted

An Essay 55

his birth; and on every side he heard conditions, policies, systems, methods, even codes of conduct and social manners, either commended as democratic or disparaged as undemocratic; and all by people who understood neither what they said, nor whereof they affirmed.

For such as these, the word "democracy" was merely the emotional expression of an irrational and extravagant political optimism, released in the eighteenth century by the French Revolution. The philosophy of this optimism, such as it was, was shaped by the speculations of Condorcet, Locke, Mme. de Staël, Rousseau, Price, Turgôt, Priestley, and in this country by those of Mr. Jefferson. In the Philadelphia of the mid-century, America was still popularly regarded as the land of political promise as well as of economic promise. Political experiments which had failed in Europe would succeed here. America's great cardinal experiment, its constitutional system, would prove beyond peradventure that the common run of Americans, high and low, rich and poor, one with another, might safely be trusted with the management of their public affairs; its success would be a brilliant and overwhelming vindication of the practicability of "democracy" as well as of its righteousness. America's great example would usher in the tenth and final epoch of human progress as envisaged by Condorcet—the epoch of international equality and of individual equality, in freedom, in opportunity, and in the exercise of natural rights; in a word, the epoch of "democracy" pure and undefiled. Mr. Jefferson's writings—albeit with occasional lapses and questionings—express this spirit of excessive hopefulness on its serious and attractive side. Dickens, who visited the United States in 1842, when Henry George was three years old, and again in 1867 when George was twenty-eight, encountered this spirit of excessive hopefulness on its serious side, and also on its fraudful and objectionable side as represented by sharking politicians and the jackals of journalism; and he recorded his impressions of both sides in a volume of travel-sketches and in a novel.

Associated with this spirit of eighteenth-century political optimism, and in large measure supporting and promoting it, was the spirit of eighteenth-century optimism concerning the moral constitution of man. Putting the doctrine roughly, George's early environment was one of sincere belief that the moral nature of man is essentially good. Like St. Paul, man always wants to be better than he is and to do better than he does; and although often led astray by "the suggestions of the flesh and of the current thoughts," by the capricious and unconsidered impulses of primitive desire, his natural disposition is to make a return upon himself and do better. Thus every man is a Jean Valjean at heart; he is indefinitely improvable; no limit can be set to anyone's potential advancement towards perfection. The current type of religion supported this optimism; *estote ergo vos perfecti* could not have been said in vain. The Rev. Josiah Jupp therefore held that if the taint of original sin has been washed away, and the benefit of the Atonement duly arranged for, this optimism is permissible and should be encouraged. Murdstone made no objection; optimism is always a good thing, it helps business and tends to keep people cheerful; therefore he went through the motions of sharing in its spirit, and perhaps, in moments of unusual exaltation, did actually share in it. Nor was this optimism confined to considerations of moral perfectibility. The American system of free public education bore witness to the optimistic belief that intellectually, also, everybody is indefinitely improvable. Mr. Creakle acquiesced in this optimism, and the discipline of Salem House reflected it to some degree; though as we have seen, its ways of reflecting it were perhaps somewhat tortuous and straitened.

In 1857 Henry George put behind him forever the civilization of Murdstone and Quinion in its most presentable and appetizing development, and went forward to associate himself with the civilization of Murdstone and Quinion in the raw. He left Philadelphia for good and all, never returning save for brief and infrequent visits with his family. He took with him, as part of the general furniture of his mind, certain postulates about the intellectual and moral constitution of man; about the political organization of society; about family life; about the nature and purpose of education. These postulates remained with him throughout his life, unchanged and apparently unexamined. He had not established them by reflective thought, but had absorbed them from his environment, as part of the air he breathed; and it does not appear that he ever questioned their validity. Thus equipped, he arrived at San Francisco on the *Shubrick,* after an uncommonly difficult and perilous voyage, on the twenty-seventh of May, 1858.

3

IN going to the coast, George had a second string to his bow; in case he did not find his everlasting fortune waiting for him in California, he thought of pushing on to Oregon, to work at printing. A family of neighbours, a widow and two daughters, had lately moved there from Philadelphia on account of a relative who had been appointed governor of Oregon Territory. George had corresponded with them, asking how things were in the printing business out there, and had got an encouraging reply. The governor said he should come, and "thinks you may do well" at printing, but would make further inquiries, and let him know definitely how his chances stood. The widow, a Mrs. Curry, with whom George did most of his corresponding, wrote that "everything pays well here," citing a chore-boy's wages of twenty dollars a month, and a ploughman's pay of twenty-five dollars for three days' ploughing. She said nothing about current prices, so George did not know whether such wages were really high or only apparently high; nor did he ask. At that time the difference between real wages and apparent wages was an obscure matter to most people, and doubtless neither George nor his correspondents had ever thought of it.

This prospect fizzled out. George took Mrs. Curry's representations on trust; he wrote her that "your statement of the prospects that I may anticipate in Oregon has decided me. I *will* go out as soon as possible." It was with this understanding that he made his way to San Francisco on the *Shubrick,* expecting to find there a letter from Mrs. Curry with further information about possible opportunities. He was disappointed; no letter awaited him, and when one came some days later, it contained no information; it was non-committal. George wrote at once a very dignified and rather pathetic missive, saying as delicately as possible that his mind was not fully made up as to what he should do, and he would be grateful for her advice. "Please write to me as soon as possible. If you still think I can do well in Oregon, I will go up as soon as I can procure my discharge from the ship." He reminded her gently that "the old Oregon fever has not entirely died, as you may judge from the fact that I write from San Francisco. I have worked hard and long to get here, and have at last succeeded." After a lapse of some five weeks, he got in reply the simple and sufficient statement, redolent of all his experience of life so far, that "as for this place, business is dull"; and that was the end of his attempts on Oregon. Later on he wrote his mother in all good humour that "letters from the Currys are getting more and more like angel's visits."

In San Francisco also, business was dull. An old pathologist, lecturing to medical students on the effect of stimulants upon the system, used to say impressively, "After stimulation, gentlemen—never forget it, never lose sight of it for a moment—after stimulation, paralysis." This sequence appears to prevail in industry as invariably as in physiology. In 1849, cooks in the restaurants of San Francisco were getting $500 a month, and there was not nearly enough of them to go around; not enough cooks, not enough restaurants, not enough of any kind of labour, shops, commodities, professional services of all sorts—not enough of anything to satisfy the existing economic demand, even at highwayman's prices. Nine years later, in 1858, in the month after George's arrival, news came that gold had been struck in British Columbia, just across the boundary, near the mouth of the Fraser; and instantly it seemed that the whole floating population of Northern California was on its way up there, taking the excess economic demand along with them. There was little doing then in San Francisco for anyone, and wages fell abruptly; labour was again in a buyer's market. George could find nothing, so he joined the rush, working his way as a sailor on a schooner bound for Victoria.

He had a cousin in San Francisco, another emigrant Philadelphian named James George, a book-keeper in a store, who thought he saw a chance to make his fortune by selling miner's supplies in Victoria. It seemed reasonable, for thousands of miners had camped there, waiting for the river-freshets to subside and uncover the diggings a hundred miles up-stream. James George went into partnership with a fruiterer in San Francisco who apparently had enough capital to swing the venture, and set up the store in Victoria, in a one-storey wooden shack; he arranged with his cousin Henry to tend the store for him during the interim of waiting for the floods to go down; and in case Henry failed to make a strike at the gold-diggings, he would give him a steady job at clerking.

This prospect also fizzled out; there was no gold to be found, worth speaking of. The camp broke up, the miners dispersed themselves, and the store went flat. Henry George had a hard life during the period of expectant waiting. He lived in a sort of attic over the store, part of the time in the store itself; doing his own cooking, what there was of it, and as he wrote his sister Jennie, "I slept rolled up in my blanket on the counter or on a pile of flour, and afterwards I had a straw mattress on some boards. The only difference between my sleeping and waking costumes was that during the day I wore both boots and cap, and at night dispensed with them."

This experience appears to have inoculated George against another run of gold-fever; he was through with mining; his only subsequent ventures in the mine-fields were purely speculative; they were also profitless and brief. He went back from Victoria to San Francisco, having borrowed enough money for a steerage-passage down. A friend gave him a coat; he had none. He reached San Francisco quite resolved, as often before, that in case nothing turned up for him ashore he would go back to following the sea. There was no opening for him at his trade of printing. He wrote home that "everything is very dull"—the old story; Murdstone's ill-running economic mechanism was on another dead-centre—but he added hopefully, "the late rains, by increasing the gold yield, will tend to make times better." Pending this improvement, he got a job as weigher in a rice-mill; and almost immediately the rice-mill shut down.

His thoughts turned then once more to the interior, where the mining districts were; having given up mining, he would try prospecting; which means finding a likely piece of unappropriated mineral territory, and filing a claim to it which could be subsequently sold—a purely speculative enterprise. About the only money left in the mining districts at the time was in this sort of wild-catting. He set off for the gold-fields, and "having no other way of reaching them," he said in later years, "I started out to walk. I was, in fact, what would now be called a tramp." It seems an insane undertaking, even for a poverty-stricken twenty-year-old boy. Along the way he did odd jobs at farm-work and whatever kind of casual toil he could get to do; he ate what was given him, and slept in barns. He did not reach the gold-fields; he gave up after a month of this exhausting life, and made his way back to San Francisco as best he might. This experience banished his last thought of quick fortune and easy money at prospecting; he wrote home that "I have given up all idea of going to the mines."

It was hard for him to face the realization that the easy money simply was no longer there; others had skimmed it all off. If he had not arrived just a shade too late, he might have had his share of luck; he might then have not only put his family safely away from the selvage-edge of destitution where they had so long clustered, but also set them up on a great height of respectability in the very best of Murdstone's civilization. How complaisantly Murdstone himself would have hobnobbed with his father after dinner of a Sunday evening in his opulent surroundings, listening to the old man's miscellaneous volubility about bygone days! How his mother would have gone in the unostentatious array of quiet elegance to call on Miss Jane Murdstone; how she would have found her sitting amidst her hard black boxes with their hard brass nails, her dress trimmed with hard black jet; and how uncompromisingly their talk would have run on the work of the Dorcas Society, the condition of the heathen, and the wicked pretensions of the Scarlet Woman on the Seven Hills! All such hopes and expectations were gone now, and it was hard to let them go; they still haunted his imagination. A year after his wretched attempt at prospecting, he wrote his sister:

> I had a dream last night, such a pleasant vivid dream that I must tell you of it. I thought I was scooping treasure out of the earth by handfuls, almost delirious with the thoughts of what I would now be able to do, and how happy we would all be; and so clear and distinct that I involuntarily examined my pockets when I got up in the morning, but alas! with the usual result.

All he could do for his family now was to suggest to this sister that she might like to go out to the coast and teach; women were scarce and much needed, their civilizing influence was greatly missed, and schoolteaching was well paid. As for himself, the cards of fate were apparently dealt down to a choice between his two trades; he could try for a chance at printing, or he could go to sea. There was always the sea, of course; it gave one a living of sorts, but its pay was poor and the life was hard; while on the other hand, printing was precarious, but if one could once get a toe-hold on it, the pay was better. He would first try his best at printing. He did so, and through the fortunate accident of stumbling on a compositor whom he had known while learning the trade in Philadelphia, he got a job worth twelve dollars a week. It was apprentice's pay, although he was twenty years old and was doing journeyman's work; union rules did not permit a minor to qualify as a journeyman. In the course of a year, however, September, 1860, he would pass his twenty-first birthday, and would then be free of his trade.

II

Nevertheless, as it turned out, being free of his trade did not improve his condition or brighten his prospects; both went steadily from bad to worse. The story of Henry George's life during the succeeding five years, from 1861 to 1865 inclusive, makes hideously depressing reading, even in the meagre outline which is all that is necessary for the purposes of this essay. He set type, first on one newspaper, then on another, as opportunity offered, but no opportunity of any kind throughout these five years held any chance of permanence. He had a brief period of prosperity at the outset, as foreman on a weekly paper at thirty dollars a week, but the paper was soon sold out from under him, and he went adrift again. He had saved a little money which he invested in a project with five other derelict printers, to get out a paper of their own. He worked at this "until my clothes were in rags, and the toes of my shoes were out. I slept in the office and did the best I could to economize, but finally I ran in debt thirty dollars for my board-bill." He and two others sold their shares in the paper to the three remaining partners, but got nothing; the paper was a failure, and the purchasers could not pay anything to anybody.

At this juncture he married a young Australian orphan; it was a runaway marriage, for the girl's guardian, her uncle, had driven him from the house after a brisk altercation, and forbade her having anything to do with him. At the time of the marriage, George had one silver coin in his possession, and even that was rightfully not his, as he had some debts. Apparently the uncle-guardian, or guardian-uncle,

An Essay

washed his hands of his niece, for although he was well-to-do, there is no record of his giving her any help in her terrible subsequent privations, or indeed of a word passing between them; they became reconciled about eight years later.

He got substitute-work as a typesetter in San Francisco, thus managing to pay board for himself and his wife; then going to Sacramento, he got a job of the same sort, living from hand to mouth. Presently he did better; for a couple of months he got from thirty-six to forty dollars a week, but only by the very hardest labour; "working steadily, and literally working all the time. . . . Had not my necessities been so great, I would not have worked as I have during that time, for no one can do so for any time and retain good health." Great indeed his necessities were, for a month after he wrote these words to his sister, his first child was born. By a rather interesting coincidence, one of the odd jobs he picked up to eke out his income at this period was an evening's work in a box-office, taking tickets for a lecture given by another derelict newspaper-man known afterwards as Mark Twain.

Being a little ahead at the end of a year, he

paid up some of his old debts in San Francisco; leaving enough of them, however, to hang over his head, with subsequent increments, for nearly twenty years. He also sank a trifle in some mining stock of the cat-and-dog variety, and lost it, thus rounding out his experience with the precious metals in the capacity of investor. After about a year of grinding hard labour to produce these results, he lost his last job in Sacramento and returned to San Francisco; his wife followed with her baby as soon as she could get ready to do so.

George found nothing to do at his trade in San Francisco; at the moment there was nothing whatever. He tried canvassing for subscribers for a newspaper that was wobbling on its feet, and he carried a side-line of clothes-wringers, but he could not get anybody interested in either; after five days of diligent tramping about from house to house, he had not netted a dozen subscribers or sold a single wringer. He did a little typesetting on the paper for which he was canvassing, but worked harder at getting his wages than he did at the type-case. He went to another paper as a substitute for a little while, and then to another, finally going into partnership with two other industrial waifs who had conceived the notion of setting up a job-printing office. He borrowed what he could for his share of financing this enterprise, and gave notes for the rest, payable out of his share of the takings; and thus at the end of 1864 he had nothing to show for three years of unceasing effort but a crushing accumulation of debts.

The job-printing enterprise was a failure; no business; the depression had set in again, this time aggravated by a great drought which prostrated mining, ranching and farming alike; which in turn took the bottom out from under all the commercial and industrial activities in California. One of George's partners dropped out. George and the other partner took twenty-five cents each out of the day's business, when there was any, to buy food; George, the partner, George's wife and baby, clubbed together in George's lodgings for such meals as they had. George could not pay his rent; he had no fire; the day after Christmas he tried at six wood-yards to get some firewood "in trade" for printing stationery, cards, labels, or what-not, but failed. His borrowing-power was used up; his wife had pawned every article of value which she had, except her wedding-ring. Twenty years afterwards he said of this period:

> I came near starving to death, and at one time I was so close to it that I think I should have done so but for the job of printing a few cards which enabled us to buy a little corn meal. In this darkest time in my life my second child was born.

It was born 27 January, 1865, a day short of one month after George's fruitless attempt to get some firewood; a month of utter destitution. He was alone in the house with his wife and the older child; there was no warmth, nothing to eat. George took the older child to a neighbour and went down to the printing-shop, hoping for some trifling order, no matter what; nothing came. He had to have money; earn it or borrow it he could not; he must beg it or steal it. Going out on the street again, he stopped a stranger and demanded five dollars. The man asked what for, and he told him. The stranger gave him the money. "If he had not," George said afterwards, "I think I was desperate enough to have killed him."

George's memoranda for the next four months are a continuous record of struggle, failure, disappointment, debt and destitution.

An Essay

In mid-February there is the abrupt entry "Am in very desperate plight." Next day, "Don't know what to do." Next day, ". . . but got no work." Early in March, 1865, he began to get some odd jobs at typesetting; he tried to get wagon-builders interested in a new type of carriage-brake which one of his acquaintances had invented; his wife meanwhile did sewing for their landlady to clear a month's rent; and thus dragging on, he did succeed in somehow keeping body and soul together.

III

There began to be borne in on George the conviction that there was something radically wrong with the machinery of Murdstone's economic system; and naturally this conviction first took shape in the belief, which never quite deserted him, that there was something essentially wrong with Murdstone. There was good ground for this; whatever way you looked at him, Murdstone was a poor figure. Not for a long time, however, did George see what under the circumstances it was by no means easy to see, that the chief count against Murdstone was not his inhumanity but his unwisdom, his appalling lack of intelligence. George William Curtis, writing the *Potiphar Papers* at about this time, had a better insight into Murdstone's qualities and conditions, and gave a fairer view of him, showing that his most conspicuous shortcomings sprang from this root of sheer intellectual incapacity, and that he too was much at the mercy of his own system, as a kind of Frankenstein. Henry George came into this view later; the working-out of his philosophy made it inevitable that he should do so; but his terrible experience of life made it perhaps as inevitable that he should always feel an involuntary ruffled impatience with Murdstone's lack of intelligence, as if it were something that Murdstone could and should outgrow or in some way make up for.

His first reaction to the grim apparition of Murdstone was emotional and superficial. He had determined to practice writing in his spare moments between typesetting and jobhunting, and he had risked sending up some trifles of anonymous copy from the composing-room, which were found printable. In one of these he fulminated against the influences which "pander to wealth and power, and would crush the poor man beneath the wheel of the capitalist's

An Essay

carriage." He inveighed against society's tendency "to resolve itself into classes who have too much or too little," and against the spirit of "quick reprobation for any effort of mechanics or labourers to obtain their dues, but nothing to say against combinations to deprive them of their rights"; and he called on "the intelligence of our class" to come forth and assert itself.

This was pure labourite separatism, expressed in standard labourite idiom—one might almost say, in standard labourite slang. It was a labourite version of the earlier Jacksonians' contention in the Philadelphia of George's boyhood, indiscriminately ranging the Have-nots against the Haves, and posing Murdstone as the incarnation of a tyrannous and oppressive "money power." The idea that natural law might be operative in the circumstances, and that Murdstone might be as helplessly victimized in the course of its operation as the poorest of the Have-nots, was entirely absent from George's reflections at this time.

George emerged from his frightful experiences in a spirit of uninformed and irrational rebellion; he was for the under dog, wherever found, and under whatever circumstances. He accepted the Civil War as purely and simply a war against slavery, and grieved that he could take no part in it; he saw it with the eyes of the most fanatical Abolitionists, as a high and holy crusade in behalf of human freedom. Of the disreputable economic designs and connivances masked by this thin pretext, he knew nothing. His fellow-newspaperman Artemus Ward, with whom he may have rubbed elbows in California, could have enlightened him; but he was in no mood to be enlightened, and Artemus Ward had too profound a knowledge of human nature to attempt it, even if the opportunity had come his way.

George was in the mood of a crusader, however, and a crusader he would be. If he could not enlist in the Civil War and crusade for the cause of anti-slavery, he would crusade for something; he would sign on for the first eligible cause that turned up—and so he did. Poor as a church mouse, in debt to his ears, with a wife and two children on his hands, and now for the first time seeing some prospect of a settled occupation, he enrolled himself in a preposterous filibustering organization called the Monroe League. The object was to go into Mexico and help the patriots under Juarez drive out the army which Louis-Napoléon had

An Essay 77

sent over to set up a puppet-state with the Austrian arch-duke Maximilian as emperor. The Monroe League fitted out an old sailing-ship and made a start, but a revenue-cutter headed them off, and the project ignominiously fell through. Years afterwards George said he now knew it "could have had no possible good end," and that some members of the expedition, in their enthusiasm, and no doubt also in their ignorance, contemplated schemes of actual piracy; indeed, half a dozen of them were put on trial as intending pirates. The League swore in its members on the emblem of a naked sword and the republican flag of Mexico; and it put the cap-sheaf on its *opera-buffa* performances by swearing in Mrs. George as its only female member!

4

IN 1866, the year following the Monroe League's escapade, George graduated up from the composing-room to the editorial department. When the report of Lincoln's assassination came in on 15 April, 1865, he had written a fiery anonymous letter which, to his surprise, his paper used as an editorial; he was then working as a substitute typesetter on the *Alta California*. It attracted attention, and he found encouragement to write odd bits on general subjects, some of them fanciful; he thought of trying his hand at a novel. His ascent of the journalistic ladder began late in 1866; he was then a compositor on the San Francisco *Times*. The editor let him combine some reporting with his typesetting, and occasionally gave him a chance to feel his feet on the editorial page. In a short time he went on as a regular editorial writer; and very soon afterwards he took charge of the paper as managing editor, at fifty dollars a week. This uncommonly rapid climb, accomplished in seven months, determined his activities for the next nine years, as those of a journalist and publicist.

It was as poor and irrelevant a novitiate for a philosopher as could well be devised. The journalist is incessantly preoccupied with what are, after all, minutiæ, and in the nature of his profession he must make as much of them as he can; hence in his own eyes they come to assume a greatly exaggerated importance. The reaction upon his mental processes is therefore dishevelling; the reflective faculty tends to atrophy from persistent disuse. It is necessary to look a little closely into George's journalistic career, first, in order to identify such permanent marks as it made on his later activities, and second, to remark the extraordinary pertinacity with which the saving instinct of the philosopher kept coming to his aid unbidden in the face of all that the practice of journalism could do to repress it. Save him whole and undamaged it did not, and could not; he did not clearly recognize it for what it was; he was quite without preparation for identifying and properly entertaining it. Mr. Creakle had not perceived the real bent of his intellectual curiosity, and his relations with Murdstone's civilization, obviously, had not been such as to disclose that bent to anyone, even to himself, and still less to afford it encouragement. Yet save him that instinct did, albeit with lamentable disfigurement; and in view of that ultimate partial triumph of instinct, costly indeed, but real, the years devoted to journalism, from 1866 to 1875, may be thought the most important of his life.

As sub-editor and managing editor of the *Times,* he was thrown into professional contact with public affairs. The spirit which he brought to this task was incongruous. As a rule, doing good is not news, and the "scheme of things entire," as presented to an editor's eye, is pretty uniformly sorry; and in consequence the editor is likely soon to grow a protective shell of cynicism. Seeing human nature and its doings chiefly by their worst and weakest side, he becomes content to let the world go its wayward course with no more than a formal and perfunctory expression of disapproval whenever the Mrs. Grundy of publishing-policy suggests that some such expression is appropriate. It is often said that the worst charge against journalism is what it makes of its servants, and in respect of encouraging a drift towards this sort of negative misanthropy, the charge seems well sustained.

George's natural temper was quick, hot, impatient; the discipline of Salem House, the hard, dogged, unyielding conventions of life in the family of a vestryman of old St. Paul's, the extremely defective type of religion and morals set forth by the Rev. Josiah Jupp, were by no means the kind of influences likely to modify it and make it amenable to the rule of reason. His more recent circumstances, such as we have seen them to be, would, if anything, tend to exacerbate it and present new objects for its exercise. Murdstone's faulty economic system had denied him all chance for fulfilment of the most moderate desires; in return for unceasing effort, endless willingness, unflagging diligence, it had all but starved him to death, and his wife and babies with him. The temptation to personalize the cause of one's afflictions is always present to human nature; he regarded Murdstone as a heartless and execrable tyrant—and even in the days of his great enlightenment, the vestiges of this repugnance never quite left him. He went into journalism in 1866, carrying the spirit of the crusading reformer; a spirit not a little unintelligent, not a little vindictive. He saw society divided into two classes, the exploiters and the exploited; himself being one of the latter class, he was uncompromisingly on its side. He was for the rescue of Murdstone's victims; he was for hitting Murdstone's head whenever it appeared; and the newspaper was his weapon.

George left the *Times* in the summer of 1868, and went as managing editor of a newspaper just starting; he lasted only a month or so at this, as he was against the paper's policy. He then went into a scheme for reviving and vitalizing a recent newspaper-venture which had more or less gone by the board. This scheme shortly petered out because it could not get a news-service; the Associated Press would not supply it. The owner sent George to New York to arrange with the Western Union Company for a competing service, but nothing could be done; the Western Union's officials were polite and pleasant, but obdurate. All George got out of the journey was a reunion with his family in Philadelphia—his first, after ten hideous years—and that was inexpressibly saddened for him because his favourite sister, Jennie, was no longer there; she died in 1862. In New York he saw a contrast between wealth and want which impressed him profoundly; his first experience in dealing with "a grinding monopoly" had put him freshly in the frame of mind to appreciate it, and besides, his ten years in California where as yet that contrast had not appeared, had increased his sensitiveness. The contrast was actually no greater than in Philadelphia, but was more conspicuous; Murdstone and Quinion had always vied with each other in making New York the stage of their most striking exhibitions. George's stay in the East lasted about five months at the most depressing time of year, giving him another disagreeable contrast with Californian conditions; he left California in December, and returned in May.

On his return, finding nothing else to do, he spent some months in miscellaneous activity; he pinch-hit at editorial writing; pinch-hit at editing an Irish Roman Catholic paper; he went back to the composing-room and set type. He could not get some $700 due him for his wages and expenses in the East; he finally sued for it. Despondency set in again; again it seemed as if Murdstone was going to be too much for him. Presently, however, he got an offer of the editorship of a paper in Oakland, across the bay; he accepted, but not for long, as once more he could not get on with the owners. He then took the editorship of a paper in Sacramento, and this connexion lasted nine months, during which, as in all his editorships, he had a fine stirring time; so much so that Murdstone, acting through the Central Pacific Railway, quietly bought the paper out from under him. His last venture was in the editorship of an evening paper which, in point of policy, was practically his own; hence it became a typical organ of "reform." It did a great deal of muckraking, handling all manner of abuses, great and small, with sensational vigour. Its independent spirit and truculent virility found a public which at the moment was much in the mood to be gratified by that sort of thing, and it became so successful that it got out a short-lived morning edition under another name. It lasted four years; then a depression came on in the wake of the great Eastern panic of the 'seventies; the mood of the paper's public changed, and George was squeezed out, too disheartened and disillusioned for any further effort. "Not caring," he said, "to ask or to receive any offer of employment from other papers, I wrote to Governor Irwin, whom I had been instrumental in electing a few months before, and asked him to give me a place where there was little to do and something to get, so that I might devote myself to some important writing. He gave

An Essay

me the office of state inspector of gas-meters, which yielded, though intermittently, a sufficient revenue to live on, and which required very little work."

II

George's editorial experience, however unsatisfactory, did not impair the overwrought expectations which he put upon the newspaper as an influence in enlightening and reshaping its readers' convictions; indeed, it seems rather to have enhanced them. Possibly it is true that this influence was more powerful in former times and in other countries than it was in his own day and place, though one can not be sure that this was ever so, and if it were, he could hardly have known of it. He appears never to have fully grasped the fact that the reading public, in its serious moments, reads newspapers only to find there its own loose prepossessions and prejudices formulated with rigour and expressed with vigour; while in its lighter moments, it reads them for entertainment; thus justifying Bishop Butler in his observation that little of our time is more idly spent than the time spent in reading. George was never far from journalism. He wrote for newspapers and periodicals all his life, as opportunity offered; twice after 1875 he had a weekly paper of his own editing. In 1879 he brought out a four-page affair called *The State* which did not live to reach a dozen issues; and in 1887, a larger and more elaborate weekly called *The Standard,* which he edited for almost four years.

George's editorial experience in the nine years ending with 1875 also confirmed him in the idea, almost universal at the time, that the quickest and best way, nay, really, the only way, to effect a reform, is through political action. With a specific reform in mind, the thing would therefore be to publicize it as widely as possible, and thrust it into politics as quickly as possible. His subsequent self-imposed discipline as a philosopher somewhat undermined his faith in this method, but such philosophical training as he was able to give himself was perforce too narrow to permit him to renounce it wholly on intellectual grounds; so while his philosophic instinct spoke out against it, his formulations were not definite enough to show him clearly why a sound instinct should do so. Emerson's saying that "the law is only a memorandum"—if, indeed, he ever met it—might have set his mind moving in another direction; so might Burke's fine saying that "there never was for any length of time a corrupt representation of a virtuous people, or a mean, sluggish, careless people who ever had a good government of any form"; so might Spencer's profound and austere observation that "there is no political alchemy by which you can get golden conduct out of leaden instincts." But the great political superstition which attributes omnipotence to legislative action held sway over the American mind. Any social end was to be gained by the passage of a law, and the final and decisive popular expression of society's need or desire was that "there ought to be a law."

As an editor, therefore, George's mind inevitably gravitated towards this superstitious view of politics. On his return from New York, after his attempts on the Associated Press and the Western Union Company, the first thing he did was to put an anti-telegraph monopoly resolution before the California legislature. It passed, but it did not enforce itself, and Murdstone probably permitted himself the luxury of a grim smile at the young editor's infatuation. Under the influence of the twin superstition about the curative properties of publicity, George had already tried to air the iniquities of the telegraph-monopoly in the press, sending a printed protest to the newspapers of New York, Philadelphia and other large Eastern cities, as well as to those of California. He had great hopes of this; he wrote a friend in California that "you will hear thunder all around the sky, notwithstanding the influence of the Western Union and the Associated Press." One New York paper printed his communication; the effect on the Western Union Company was as little noticeable as the effect on public sympathy; no one heard any thunder anywhere. George's attacks on the Californian railway-and-express monopolies, published in the New York *Tribune*, were no more effective; they merely got him blacklisted in the *Tribune* office. The paper had contracted with him for some letters describing the route of the great new transcontinental railway. He was to write these letters on his return over the route; he wrote some of them, sent them in, but the new managing editor, Whitelaw Reid, refused to print them and annulled the contract out of hand. Such were the uses of publicity, such was the practical upshot of the superstition about

An Essay

it as an instrument of reform; a superstition which lurked in the depths of George's *Unbewusstsein* all his days, long after it had been exploded by the operations of his conscious mind. At this time he did not question it, he believed in it implicitly. With what superior worldly-wisdom might Murdstone, if they had been on speaking terms, have taken the young man aside and reminded him of Frederick the Great's saying to another impetuous reformer, "Ah, my dear Sulzer, you don't know this damned human race."

Full of the ardour fomented by these twin superstitions, George tried twice to enter the California legislature. The first time, in 1869, he did not get the nomination; the second time, two years later, he was nominated on the heels of an anti-railway governor who was up for re-election, wearing the Democratic label. George acted as secretary of the convention that year. The whole ticket went to defeat in a landslide. In 1872 he was elected a delegate to the Democratic national convention at Baltimore, which nominated Horace Greeley. He subsequently got the Democratic nomination to the constitutional convention in California, but failed of election. His whole career as a seeker after elective office in California was that of an also-ran. His party-title was Democratic. All the newspapers he served were Democratic. Civil-War Republicanism was one thing; the best traditions of Philadelphia were in its favour; but the Republicanism of special interests, high tariffs and carpet-baggery was quite another thing, forcing him to conclude that the Republican party, as he saw its performances under Grant (for whom he had voted in 1868), "had served its purpose." In all this he did not perceive that the so-called party-system in government is the fruit of one of Murdstone's happiest inspirations; permitting, as it does, the specious and attractive promise of a reform in flagitious governmental policies and practices, without the performance. Indeed, George never did clearly perceive this, although his philosophical instinct gave him the strongest possible intimations of it in later life. Cleveland's second administration brought him almost in full view of it, but not quite; one could not say that he ever actually took it in.

George fought all manner of battles during his connexion with the editorial side of journalism, but it might be said of him as an old legend said of the Irish, that "they went forth to the wars, but they always fell." The most conspicuous instance of his being on the winning side was one where he showed what appears at first sight to be a rather striking reversal of form; this was in his vigorous support of excluding Chinese immigration. In an article written to influence Eastern opinion, he gave an extremely bad account of the Chinese immigrants, as "utter heathens, treacherous, sensual, cowardly and cruel. . . . Their moral standard is as low as their standard of comfort. . . . They practice all the unnamable vices of the East, . . . generally apparently cleanly, but filthy in their habits. Their quarters reek with noisome odours, and are fit breeding-places for pestilence."

From what is known about our Chinese settlers at the present time, this seems somewhat *ex parte*. One might suppose, on the other hand, that it may mean no more than that the immigrants in George's day were an uncommonly bad lot, and that George's error lay in bringing an indictment against a whole nation on the strength of a very inferior sample. Mark Twain, however, who encountered those same Chinese, and who was as keen an observer as George, gives a totally different account of them; and he too wrote with a view to Eastern opinion. He devoted a whole chapter of *Roughing It* to showing that the Chinese were quite what we know them to be today, and ends by saying:

> They are a kindly-disposed, well-meaning race, and are respected and well-treated by the upper classes, all over the Pacific Coast. No Californian gentleman or lady ever abuses or oppresses a Chinaman under any circumstances; an explanation that seems to be much needed in the East. Only the scum of the population do it, they and their children; they and, naturally and consistently, the policemen and politicians likewise, for these are the dust-licking pimps and slaves of the scum, there as elsewhere in America.

The longer acquaintance which the country has had with its Chinese immigrants would suggest that this account is the more nearly accurate. George said many years afterwards that his account was "crude," because he "had not then come to clear economic views"; but it does not appear that he ever changed his attitude towards the main issue. In considering his attitude, it must be borne in mind that exclusion of the Chinese was a labour-measure; the hated

An Essay

monopolists were large employers of low-grade labour, and organized labour feared that Chinese competition would drive wages down. Race-hatred and race-prejudice were the consequence, as they invariably are; there is no known instance of their appearance except where the fear of some form of economic undercutting is present. The labour-issue in California was clearly drawn and deep-cut; it was fought out with all the reckless and passionate violence of the untamed frontier; and George was unreservedly on the side of labour. His early anonymous contributions to the papers he worked for were signed "Proletarian." In the immense excitement over the news that the transcontinental railway was really a fact and not a dream, "after we had shouted ourselves hoarse, I began to think, what good is it going to be to men like me; to those who have nothing but their labour? I saw that thought grow and grow." How far indeed this narrow and sectarian class-concept had to grow, how broadly it had to expand, before the same man could take his stand before an audience and extemporize such an introduction as: "Ladies and gentlemen, I am not for the poor man. I am not for the rich man. I am for man."

III

It grew in a curious fashion. While George was fighting the battle of life as a reforming and crusading editor, pillorying all the abuses which he associated with Murdstone's growing power; while he was supporting the cause of labour at the risk of justice; wholly committed to an irrational faith in political action and involved in the tortuous course of political partisanship: a purblind instinct was working in direct opposition to everything he was doing and believing. It was working to take his attention off the supposititious villainy of Murdstone, and fasten it on the weaknesses of Murdstone's economic system; to show him that the aims of labour were wrongly directed, that persistence in them was ruinous, and that, strictly speaking, there is no such thing as a labour-issue—that if Murdstone's system were revamped and put in proper working-order, every so-called labour-problem would disappear; that reliance on a tendentious vehement publicity is self-defeating; that political action is in its nature a preposterously ineffectual instrument of reform, and that faith in it is a benumbing and degrading superstition.

An Essay

One may say, putting it broadly, that George was unconscious of this instinct's working; that is, he did not recognize the instinct for what it was. All the conditions and circumstances of his life conspired with his natural temper to militate against that clear recognition. This need not have been so; one sees with infinite regret how slight an initial change in his circumstances was needed to avert it; above all, how little insight on the part of Mr. Creakle was needed to avert it. In 1877 George told a story of his boyhood which to any reflecting person must seem the most terrible indictment ever penned against the discipline of Salem House:

When I was a boy I went down to the wharf with another boy to see the first iron steamship which had ever crossed the ocean to our port. Now, hearing of an iron ship seemed to us then a good deal like hearing of a leaden kite or a wooden cooking-stove. But we had not long been aboard of her before my companion said in a tone of contemptuous disgust, "Pooh, I see how it is; she's all lined with wood. That's the reason she floats."

I could not controvert him for the moment, but I was not satisfied, and sitting down on the wharf when he left me, I set to work trying mental experiments. If it was the wood inside of her that made her float, then the more wood the higher she would float; and mentally I loaded her up with wood. But as I was familiar with the process of making boats out of blocks of wood, I at once saw that instead of floating higher, she would sink deeper. Then I mentally took all the wood out of her, as we dug out our wooden boats, and saw that, thus lightened, she would float higher still. Then in imagination I jammed a hole in her, and saw that the water would run in and she would sink, as did our wooden boats when ballasted with leaden keels. And thus I saw as clearly as though I could have actually made these experiments with the steamer, that it was not the wooden lining that made her float, but her hollowness; or, as I would now phrase it, her displacement of water.

One asks oneself in amazement how it was possible for Mr. Creakle ever to miss perceiving the bent of a mind like this; and having perceived it, how he could fail to encourage it to the utmost and help create circumstances for its free and undisturbed development. This very moderate amount of insight, however, lay far outside the scholastic equipment of Salem House, far outside George's whole intellectual

An Essay

environment, early or late. The predominance of the philosophical instinct effected itself gradually, and against all the force of wind and tide. The instinct abdicated at intervals throughout his life, it never scored a complete and lasting triumph, but when one sees what its power and persistence was, and considers the crushing forces which were massed against it, one's emotion falls but little short of reverent wonder.

The first instance where this instinct emerged and took charge of his mental processes on a matter of public policy was not long after he arrived in California. He was then a protectionist, or thought he was, though he had never examined the subject. He said he "had accepted the belief, as in the first place we all accept our beliefs, on the authority of others"; back in Philadelphia his entourage had had it straight from Murdstone that one should be a protectionist. George said further that he remembered how logically he had thought the Confederate cruisers' raids on merchant shipping were a good thing because they gave California the equivalent of a high protective tariff against Eastern industries, thus raising wages and increasing the demand for labour; perfectly good sound doctrine from Murdstone's point of view. Presently, though, he heard a very able debater give the arguments for protectionism, and they made him a free-trader on the spot. If what the debater said were true, it would logically follow "that the country that was hardest to get at must be the best country to live in; and that instead of merely putting duties on things brought from abroad, we ought to put them on things brought from anywhere; and that fires and wars and impediments to trade and navigation were the very best things to levy on commerce."

George's editorial experience brought him face to face with an accumulation of public questions, each of which seemed universally to be regarded as individual, distinct, unrelated; they were not synthesized under any general philosophy of social organization. The Chinese question stood by itself; so did slavery; so did protectionism; so did unemployment; so did the recurrence of industrial depression; so did the wage-question; and so on. Politics, by fastening now on one and now on another of these questions and bruiting them vociferously abroad before the public as "issues," confirmed the tendency to regard each one as a special thing, to be dealt with specifically. Journalism did likewise. It did not occur to anyone, apparently, to suspect that they might all alike be symptomatic of one fundamental and general disorder, and that they might be correlated accordingly.

This suspicion did not occur to George. In his nine years of editing he too, as much as anyone, had treated each of these public questions as an end in itself. Like any honest editor, he must have felt a vague dissatisfaction at observing that such treatment, even if apparently successful, led only to the raising up of new and unsuspected difficulties, each one in its turn to be posed as an unrelated public question, an unrelated "issue"; and so there was nothing in the method of crusading reform but the prospect of everlasting warfare. Slavery could be abolished *vi et armis,* and so it was; but what then? Telegraph-monopoly might be abolished; but what then? Free trade might supplant protection out of hand; but what then?

George did not rationalize his dissatisfaction in this way, nor could he have done so at the time; his preparation was inadequate to that. The philosophical instinct asserted itself only in setting the dissatisfaction alight and keeping its irritating flame alive. Out of editing and out of politics; still miserably poor, but with the reasonable prospect of two years' bare living out of a minor political sinecure: he reviewed some of the public problems which had borne so heavily upon him all his life. He considered them with the same philosophical simplicity and directness which he had applied in his boyhood to the problem of the iron ship. In Philadelphia, when he was eighteen, an old printer had told him that in old countries wages are always low, and always high in new countries. He had often recalled that remark, and wondered why it was so; now he would really try to get to the ground of that phenomenon, and find out. A year later, on a topsail schooner carrying him up the coast to his ill-fated storekeeping venture in Victoria, he had heard a miner say that wages would not always be as high in California; "as the country grows, as people come in, wages will go down." He had remembered that also, observed that it was true, and wondered at it. Why should the mere increase of population have that effect, as obviously it did have? Everybody was hoping to see the country grow, everybody devoutly believed that the increase of population was a good thing, everybody was strong for attracting population, all California was half out of its mind at the prospect of a transcontinental railway because it would bring people in; yet since the overwhelming majority of Californians worked for wages, and since the increase of population drove wages down, how could that increase be a good thing for California? He had asked that question casually, but the answers struck him as no better than the boy's theory of the steamship's wooden lining. He would dig around the roots of that matter, and see what they looked like. Again, he had been born in a depression, and wherever he went, depressions had relentlessly dogged his footsteps; why should there be depressions, and why did they so regularly recur? In the nature of things there seemed no reason for them; the country was rich enough to keep its thin straggling population busy as nailers all the time, and support them handsomely. He had thought, as anybody might, that there was something wrong with Murdstone's system which might account for them, but he had not set himself to discover what was wrong, and why. After seeing the show of poverty and riches which Murdstone and Quinion had put on in New York, he was tempted to think that Murdstone had deliberately planned his economic mechanism to work that way, though he had not seen precisely how he did it. As an editor and publicist-politician, he had hammered Murdstone hard on general principles, but without knowledge of how much blame to assess him, or of the actual reasons for assessing him any blame; he merely followed the immemorial practice of editors and politicians. He would now do his best to temper that practice by injecting into it as much sound knowledge as he could acquire, and as much close reasoning as he could devise.

IV

He had already put his finger on what he thought to be one defect in Murdstone's economic system, namely: its sanction of the monopoly of land. His attention had been attracted to this by the rapid growth of huge holdings all around him; holdings which had been given away into private ownership through California's land-policy, which in reckless prodigality was equalled only by that of the nation at large. There was a land-rush towards the prospective railway-terminal as eager as the earlier gold-rush towards the mines; the land-grants owned by the railway itself were enormous. This made talk; disaffected persons thought this wholesale surrender of territory into the hands of the railway-monopoly was bad, and they said so. George was one of them; his wrath at the railway-company's greed and ruthlessness—added to his conviction that its project boded no good "to men like me; to those who have nothing but their labour"— sharpened his scent for its iniquities. In 1871, therefore, he published a small pamphlet which he entitled *Our Land and Land-Policy, National and State*.

His approach to the subject was once more the approach of a philosopher, direct, simple and logical. Man is a land-animal; he derives his sustenance only from the land; and if he be deprived of access to land, he perishes. Land is one of nature's free gifts, and each one has a right to the use of so much of it as may be needful for supplying all the wants of his existence, in so far as is consistent with maintaining the equal rights of others. The right to property in land differs wholly from the right to labour-made products, inasmuch as land is not a product of labour. "To permit one man to monopolize the land from which the support of others is to be drawn, is to permit him to appropriate their labour." Therefore a just and equitable land-policy would be to "charge the expense of government upon our lands."

Philosophical though its approach was, the pamphlet was unsatisfactory, and George felt it to be so. He knew it was not only an inadequate expression of what he wished to drive at, but an imperfect expression, an illiterate expression. He simply did not know enough to manage his task competently; he knew no economics, knew nothing of the history of his subject; his mind was moving in a mist towards something uncertainly and vaguely apprehended. Yet by thus feeling his way, he had gone a surprisingly long step forward. His premises were correct; he had a clear glimpse of the true law of wages; and he had a strong intimation that there is a causal relation between land-monopoly and the aggregate of all that is, or can be, comprised in the so-called labour-problem.

So far, his findings, needless to say, were all original, all arrived at by sheer force of logical inference based on observation; but they were by no means new. Others had made the same observations, drawn the same inferences, and had presented their findings in a more orderly

An Essay

and accurate phraseology; some had gone even farther, arriving at particularized conclusions which George was not to reach until considerably later. In America, the doctrine that the earth belongs only "in usufruct" to those who live on it, had long since been laid down by Mr. Jefferson; a doctrine which he said, "I suppose to be self-evident." Paine elaborated it as George did, drawing the same distinction between law-made property and labour-made property; and instead of George's ambiguous phraseology about "land-taxation" and charging "the expense of government upon our lands," Paine introduced the clear and correct term "ground-rent"; and instead of incurring the confiscatory implications of George's word "tax," he puts it precisely that ground-rent is a debt which every landed proprietor owes to the community, thus leaving clear the distinction between taxing (which in theory may or may not bear on production, but in practice invariably does) and rent-collecting, which does not bear on production. George was vaguely aware of some such distinction, and felt for it fumblingly and in many words; Paine put it clearly in two dozen words. The perception of ground-rent as in its nature public property appears in William Penn and Peter Stuyvesant; and by a remarkable coincidence, such as occurred between Darwin and Wallace, a few months before George published his pamphlet an humble tailor in Wisconsin, named Edwin Burgess, wrote a series of letters to a newspaper in Racine, in which he made a complete anticipation of George's final proposals for the communal appropriation of economic rent.

In the Eastern hemisphere George had a long line of anticipators, partial or complete, general or special. In 1850 his Jeffersonian doctrine of natural rights went forth to the world anew under the great name of Spencer, for all time the mighty Vauban of individualism. In England, James Mill, Adam Smith and Thomas Spence; in Scotland, Patrick Edward Dove and William Ogilvie, professor at Aberdeen; in mediæval China, the autocratic political reformer Yang-Yen; in Germany, Held, Arnd, Gossen; in France, the school called the *Économistes,* or more commonly called the Physiocrats, which included Quesnay, du Pont de Nemours, Turgôt and the elder Mirabeau; all these were forerunners of George, and their anticipations of his doctrine were extremely close. He took no economic position but that can be traced back to one or another of them, often to all. The correspondences between his work and Dove's are especially remarkable; Dove published his *Theory of Human Progression* in 1850, and its resemblances to George's work were so many and so lifelike as to lead to a highly plausible but wholly baseless charge of wholesale plagiarism being brought against George in 1889, when his popularity and reputation were perhaps at their peak—or perhaps better, if one can set a time to it, when they were beginning to go rapidly downward to obscurity.

George knew nothing of all this; he wrote under no informative influence except the influence of what he saw going on immediately around him. His pamphlet represented observations on local circumstances and proposals for local application. He did not know that anyone had made precisely similar observations elsewhere, or had offered similar proposals. Such reading as he had done was not in that line; the literature of the subject was probably little available, nor would he have been likely to turn to it. When he returned to San Francisco from Victoria at the age of nineteen, there was a copy of Adam Smith's *Wealth of Nations* on the shelves in his boarding-house, but though he read most of the books there, he did not read it; in fact, strange as it seems, though after 1875 he had glanced at Smith here-and-there for reference-purposes, he did not actually read him until 1883. Apparently the only reading in economics that he did before the publication of his pamphlet was in John Stuart Mill's treatise; he looked into this while East in 1869, to see what Mill had to say on the subject of wages—it was a matter of reading-up or "cramming" for an article he wrote for the New York *Tribune*. He was always a desultory reader, having never been taught the art and practice of reading; the discipline of Salem House assumed that when one could make one's way with reasonable speed and accuracy down a printed page, one could read, and there was nothing more to be done about it. Mr. Creakle had laid the entire country under the monstrously erroneous belief that any and every literate person can read; and George was a victim of that widespread persuasion.

V

George published his pamphlet in 1871; he gave up regular newspaper-work in 1875. In the intervening years he added to his equipment as a publicist by cultivating his gifts as a public speaker. He had done a little with it before, in a small way, enough to get more or less used to thinking on his feet, and he rather liked it; besides, now that he had made sure of himself as a writer, he thought it would be a good thing to have at command another effective instrument for impressing the public. Physically, his stage-presence was not striking; he was somewhat undersized, quite bald, with a reddish beard, blue eyes, and a reflective expression. His voice was clear and strong, but pitched unpleasantly high when out of control, and always without any especially attractive musical quality; and his articulation became, with practice, so good that his words could be understood without trouble under ordinary conditions. He had imagination enough to make him, in the best sense, an accomplished rhetorician, able to touch off the enthusiasm of an audience at will; he could have been a great orator of the type of Patrick Henry, relying on sound and style for his effects, rather than on sense and substance. As it was, he became one of the most powerful public speakers of his time. The London *Times,* by no means a prejudiced witness, made him out as quite the equal of England's foremost masters in the art of swaying a popular audience, Richard Cobden and John Bright.

In a very real sense, George's conspicuous success in public speaking was a misfortune, for it tended to confirm him in his sense of himself as a man with a preaching mission as well as a philosophic mission, thus heightening his inveterate confusion of the two. Everything which strengthened his urge to spread the Light, to persist in his career as a crusading reformer, a witness-bearer before the multitude, inevitably weakened and repressed the philosophic instinct's clear intimations of what his rightful mission was and of the course he might rightfully take with it; and of all such influences the most potent one, probably, was released by his extraordinary achievements in the field of public speaking.

In 1876 George made a number of speeches; he stumped the state for Tilden in the Presidential election which seated Hayes that year. He also gave a lecture at the University of California. In this way he got his name up, and in the following year he did still more speech-making and lecturing. His political sinecure of

An Essay

inspecting gas-meters was on a fee-basis, and no longer gave him a living. Whether he had inspected all the meters and thus worked himself out of a job, or whatever the reason was, he found himself considerably in debt; so he took to lecturing in order to eke out his income. In these discourses he took up various aspects of the subject he had treated in his pamphlet of 1871—the subject of what he still loosely called land-monopoly—and thus was continually finding that each one of these aspects, in its relation to the others, would bear much closer inspection than he had given it, and consequently that there was much more to be said on the subject as a whole than he had thought there was.

Hence his dissatisfaction with his pamphlet grew. Towards the end of the year an association of about thirty men was formed in San Francisco to discuss the subject-matter of George's pamphlet, and these discussions helped both to increase George's dissatisfaction and to enlarge the scope of his view. Unfortunately the group at once also took on a proselytizing function, determined that "something must be done about it," which meant, and in the American mind could mean, nothing else but carrying George's doctrine straightway into politics, half-baked. The group organized itself as the Land Reform League of California, announcing its purpose under a misleading and mischievous description, as "the abolition of land-monopoly." It operated for a time in the futile fashion of Adullamite juntas, and then disintegrated; it was the first of many such to follow.

George lectured under the auspices of the League during 1878, speaking with great emotional force; on the platform he was the embodiment of militancy, comminatory, truculent, purposing first to arouse his hearers' sense of outrage, meanwhile informing them as he went along. He denounced Murdstone with all the vigour of impassioned rhetoric, driving hard at "the selfish greed that seeks to pile fortune on fortune, and the niggard spirit that steels the heart to the wail of distress," and asking, "Shall the ploughers forever plough the backs of a class condemned to toil? Shall the millstones of greed forever grind the faces of the poor?" His rhetoric was magnificent, superb; when one reckons in the carrying power of absolute unquestionable disinterestedness which alike pervaded and enforced it, one may safely say that its like has never been heard in America before

An Essay

or since. Yet in addition to the main point of fiscal reform which he wished to impress upon his audiences, his rhetoric withal conveyed certain adumbrations of further facts and relations which as yet he did not clearly perceive. While he was absorbed in himself as an agitator, prophet, reformer, coryphæus and herald of a new dispensation, the philosophical instinct was nudging his prepossession with poor and feeble but unmistakable suggestions of another mission which was really his; and for a time the instinct half-prevailed. He never wholly gave himself up to it, but sometimes, as now, he let it have its way provisionally, on the strict understanding that its workings should remain ancillary to his own interpretation of the main purpose of his life.

He was dissatisfied with his pamphlet from the time of its publication. Further thought, discussion, the half-heeded intimations of instinct, had opened many unsuspected gateways of investigation. He must write more; another pamphlet, or perhaps a magazine-article, approaching his subject of "land-monopoly" by way of the phenomenon of industrial depressions. He would try to answer two questions, no more; first, What is the actual cause of recurrent industrial depressions?; second, Why is it that increase of wealth is invariably accompanied by increase of want? As far as he knew, no one had yet answered these questions or even made a respectable attempt to do so. All the answers he had heard or heard of were superficial and incompetent; one might as well go back to the Rev. Josiah Jupp's hypothesis, and be done with it. Those social disabilities exist because God wants them to—that explanation at least had the merit of being fundamental and competent, if one agreed to accept it as true. George decided to see what he could do in the way of a better answer. Instinct had somehow managed to get into his head the bare unrecognized suspicion that natural law operates as inexorably in the realm of economics as it does in physics; and instinct now brought this suspicion to the front, and moved him to make it the guiding principle of his projected work.

As soon as he had sketched out his task, he saw that it was a large order, much larger than he thought; yet it had to be done. If he were to be the preacher of a social gospel, that gospel must be formulated with full account of all its ramifications, and it must be air-tight. This

An Essay

meant that he must for the time being interrupt his career of evangelizing and become *ad hoc* a philosopher. He accordingly did so; during the next eighteen months—from September, 1877, to March, 1879, inclusive—he produced the book which he entitled *Progress and Poverty*.

It is today, in point of circulation, the most successful book on economics ever printed; its sales have run to a total of more than two million copies. In two respects it is unique in economic literature; it is the first and only serious attempt to establish the cause of industrial depressions, and the cause of involuntary poverty; and it is the only book of which the author could say after eighteen years of white-hot controversy, that he had not seen a single objection to any position taken in the book which had not been fully met and answered in the book itself. Its reasoning has never been successfully impugned, and its economic premises are of course beyond question; they are a matter of common observation, common knowledge. Count Tolstoy said most truly that "people do not argue with the teaching of George; they simply do not know it: and it is impossible to do otherwise with his teaching, for he who becomes acquainted with it cannot but agree."

5

IN the eighteen months devoted to writing this book, the deadening pressure of poverty and debt never for a moment lightened. In a letter to his sister Jennie, written fifteen years before, he had asked in a moment of bitterness why one should "wonder that men lust for gold and are willing to give almost anything for it, when it covers everything; the purest and holiest desires of their hearts, the exercise of their noblest powers." One would be glad to get away from the struggle which civilization imposes and rehabilitate oneself in solitude on some isolated hillside, "but, alas, money, money is wanted, even for that." He understood this better now, if possible, than when he wrote those words. His family had increased by two; he had a wife and four children; he had before him a colossal and prospectively unremunerative undertaking, something which no one had ever even approached; yet something which must be done, for every day it was delayed, uncounted thousands of miserable beings like himself were devoured by the insatiable demon of involuntary poverty.

It is impossible to overestimate the influence of poverty in determining the course of George's career. One can account in a sentence for every puzzling and lamentable anomaly which his career presents; he had the mind of a philosopher, a philosophic mind surpassed in power but by one or two in his generation, and an expository faculty surpassed by none; but the *temperament* of a philosopher he never had. He was no Hegel, nor yet was he a Plato, born with a clear-headed sense for the appraisal of things-as-they-are, unimpressionable and free from illusions. But this judgment, while competent, is general; to be quite just, one must also give full weight to the course of circumstances which tended so powerfully to enhance that temperament and make it actually the controlling factor in the direction of his life; and of all those circumstances the most constant, indomitable and inflaming was his poverty. The dismal, illiberal life of Murdstone's social coterie in Philadelphia; the tepid and stuffy domesticity of a vestryman's family; Salem House and Mr. Creakle; the dismal, illiberal religion preached by the Rev. Josiah Jupp; the highly dubious estimate put upon the intellectual capacity and the moral nature of mankind; the untempered association with a narrow provincialism and participation in its fantastic assumptions concerning "democracy"; the narrow views of life and limited demands on life begotten of a journalistic and oratorical experience on the frontier; the incursions into practical politics: all these influences diligently fostered a temperament naturally incompatible with the abilities of a philosopher, but the one which had most to do with keeping that temperament in its ascendency was poverty.

II

Writing a book is one thing, and getting it published is another; getting it read is still another. A philosopher who knows so much about human life that he knows how little of it is worth minding, is rather indifferent to the written record. A Socrates, a Jesus, writes nothing, talks a little here and there, and leaves to others the making of a record of what he says, if any is to be made. A Marcus Aurelius scribbles a few notes, purely as memoranda for his own use and guidance, and they are preserved to us by sheer accident; others have written more extensively, and then contentedly left their work at death, to be published or remain unpublished, as any who might be interested should see fit. The complete philosopher—the philosopher by temperament as well as by intellect—does not put any extravagant expectations on either the general capacity or the general will to accept discipleship, nor indeed does he think much about it. His business is with the construction and formulation of a doctrine; its propagation is not his business.

Far otherwise is it with one who, like George, has the intellect of a philosopher and the temperament of a propagandist, especially when he has the added gifts of a superb writer and an accomplished public speaker. The doctrine once formulated, "the intimations of the dæmon" are never enough to secure him against a superheated concern with its acceptance. When he stands forth either to recommend or defend his doctrine, they are never enough, in Disraeli's fine phrase, to secure him against becoming inebriated by the exuberance of his own verbosity. This inebriety always to some extent distorts his view of the effect produced by his efforts; sometimes the distortion is monstrous and fantastic, as when he mistakes the enthusiasm of the moment for a considered and rational approval, or as when he misapprehends a purely adventitious personal popularity, and takes it as testimony to the popularity of his doctrine. As has been said, *Progress and Poverty* had a sale running into the millions; yet in all probability it never once occurred to Henry George to wonder how many of those millions of copies were ever read.

III

In March, 1879, George sent his manuscript to the firm of Appleton, in New York, who promptly and politely declined to publish it. Their rejection of it was not unreasonable, for times were frightfully bad, and in a period of depression book-buying is almost the first activity to dwindle, and quite the last to recover. Logically it should be the time when everybody would buy a book on the cause of industrial depressions, but book-buying, like most activities of old Frederick's *verdammte Rasse,* does not go by logic. Moreover, the Appletons faced a grim precedent; no book on political economy published in America had ever paid. George set friends in New York to work on the flinty hearts of other publishers, but without success; no one would touch it or have anything to do with it.

George then determined to publish the book himself, by subscription at three dollars a copy; he put out a prospectus and got some money, not enough to pay the cost of an edition, but enough, as he judged, to go on with. The circumstances of the book's publication were as pathetic as those of its writing. Hard as times were in the East, they were almost harder in California; George said later that he "could hardly walk a block without meeting a citizen begging for ten cents." An old partner in the printing business, however, who now had a shop of his own, agreed to make the stereotype plates. As a matter of sentiment, George set the first two stickfuls of type himself; the rest of the time while the plate-making was going on, like an honest author, he devoted to a final currycombing of his manuscript before it should be irretrievably out of hand.

He thus got out an "author's edition" of five hundred copies, and sold a good many of them. Meanwhile he sent unbound sheets to every likely publishing-house in England and America, proposing to furnish the plates—by far the largest item of expense in publishing any book —if they would print and bind an edition and put it on the market. He got one favourable reply; only one; the Appletons agreed to print and distribute the book on those terms. They did so. They could not get concurrent publication in England; they told George it was not necessary to reserve the rights of translation since no one would want to translate it. Nevertheless, they loyally went ahead and published the book in January, 1880; and it fell from the Appletons' presses as dead as Julius Cæsar. In the course of the year it got excellent notices in the American press; the Belgian economist de Laveleye praised it warmly in the *Revue Scientifique;* the Appletons brought it out in a cheap paper edition; it was translated into German; and still it did not sell. As compared with previous works on political economy it did perhaps as well as could be expected: but authors measure the success of a book by the number of its readers; publishers, by the volume of its sales; and measured either way, the success of *Progress and Poverty* was not encouraging.

George's long task was done, but he still had to live; his family also had to live. A friend in New York had written him that there was a fair

An Essay

chance for him on the New York *Herald* and had sent him his railway-fare, so East he went in the late summer of 1880, leaving his family behind. The place on the *Herald* was a will-o'-the-wisp, like so many others that had lured him. He landed in New York as a mere adventurer, a waif, "afloat at forty-two," he wrote a friend, "poorer than at twenty-one. I do not complain, but there is some bitterness in it." Again he was looking for work, any kind of work, while back in California his wife was taking in boarders and his older son was working in a printing-office.

He found nothing to do at writing, but one of three friends, the only ones he had in New York, got him a long list of engagements to go on the stump for the Democratic party in the Garfield-Hancock campaign. He made one speech somewhere out of town, and queered his pitch so effectively that the committee recalled him post-haste to New York, and earnestly entreated him not to make any more speeches. The Republicans had thrown the tariff-issue into the campaign, stigmatizing the Democrats as free-traders, and as George put it, what the Democrats were after "was somebody to tell the workingmen that the Democratic party was as good as the Republican party for the tariff." The speaker preceding George made that kind of speech, and George followed with a fervent plea for straight free trade. He said he had heard of high-tariff Democrats and revenue-tariff Democrats, but there was still another kind of Democrat, and that was a no-tariff Democrat; he was of that kind; he believed that what was wanted was "to sweep away the customhouses and custom-house officers, and have free trade." The audience, he said, applauded this, but the eminent Democrats on the platform went into a dreadful dither, and George took leave of them "without a man to shake my hand."

This incident is worth great attention, piled as it was immediately on top of his experience of practical politics and the party-system in the West. It is quite justly made the stock example of George's magnificent integrity, his uncompromising faithfulness to principle. It is all that; but it must also raise in any reflective mind the question, How in the world could a man of such extraordinary philosophic powers survive all that experience and still retain a shred of confidence in political action as an instrument of social improvement? He had gone into the

An Essay

Hayes-Tilden campaign, assuring his audiences that the contest was "not a contest for spoils, in which the people are simply permitted to choose which gang shall plunder them," and afterwards saw that it was exactly what he said it was not. He saw also that this had been the precise upshot—no one ever described it better—of the party-system in every local and state election in which he had taken part; and now came this experience when he was on the stump for Hancock! It is hardly conceivable that he should not have had some inkling of the fact that Murdstone invented the party-system with this end, and no other, in view, and that his faith in political action, political institutions and political men, should not be correspondingly modified. One might even suppose that he would have applied his lively intellectual curiosity and his almost unparalleled ability to the relatively simple task of getting down under the superficial appearance of these institutions and questioning their actual nature and intention. The average man, as Murdstone well knew, would not, and could not, do this; but George was not an average man.

His failure to do this had a profound practical significance; it undermined him ruinously at every point. Warnings and intimations appeared in all the circumstances of his later career; he saw them and brushed them by. Instinct spoke out loudly; sometimes he unwittingly followed its dictates a little way, but in the end repressed them and turned back. His faith seems always to have remained the sheer superficial *Aberglaube* of the reformer, expecting impossible results from this-or-that nostrum or combination of nostrums aimed at special and symptomatic disorders—nostrums like "putting good men in office" or "turning the rascals out," which were much in vogue with the insipid spirit of reform that was then at large. George was much disgusted when the eminent man of science, E. L. Youmans, the foremost American interpreter of Spencer, told him he did not vote because it was not worth while; George was caustic with Youmans, but did not let the incident suggest the advisability of examining Youmans's position disinterestedly to see what might be in it, and why; he acted only on the arbitrary and purely authoritarian dictum of the average man inspired by Murdstone, that it is the duty of every citizen to vote. He would have made nothing of the great saying of Socrates, when rebuked for taking no part in Athenian politics, that this showed only that he and his followers were the very best politicians in Athens.

George touched on political matters in his various writings, and all he said reflects this unexamined, unrationalized *Aberglaube* which ran back to two roots; first, the theory of the State as a social institution originating in some form of social agreement or contract for social purposes; and second, the prevailing theory of the moral nature of mankind—the perfectionist theory of Condorcet in popular form, powerfully reinforced and backed by the theological constructions of the Rev. Josiah Jupp. These two theories George seems never to have questioned; he had a period of youthful revulsion from the ancillary constructions of the Rev. Josiah Jupp, but it did not last long, nor did it at all affect his faith in the perfectionist thesis. What is the history of the State; in what did it invariably originate; what invariable intention and purpose has it expressed; what invariable intention does it now express wherever it exists; what inference can be drawn concerning its nature, and what concerning the individual's appropriate attitude and relation to it?—these questions apparently never occurred to George's mind. Perhaps the coöperation of the *Zeitgeist* was needed to bring them forward, and that George did not have. Again, has experience so far given any reasonable assurance that the perfectionist theory of man's moral and intellectual nature is sound? Does it encourage any reasonable expectation that the average man has either the capacity or the desire to make much more of himself in a moral or intellectual way than he ever did make or is now making? George did not consider these questions; in all probability they never occurred to him. He demonstrated clearly enough that under the present economic system the average man could not be expected to do much with himself in those ways, but he seems never to have doubted either his capacity or desire; on the contrary, he firmly assumed that he had both.

With these convictions, George was an ardent republican; he could not possibly have been anything else. If the average man is economically free, his political and social freedom follow automatically. In that freedom, and in that only, he is able to become as wise and as good as he can be and wishes to be. So far, George's reasoning was sound beyond doubt or question; the thing hangs only on the degree of wisdom and goodness that, under those vastly improved conditions, the average man would or could set for himself to reach. Assuming, as George did, that the average man's powers and desires are indefinitely greater than his present showing makes them appear to be, then it is presumable that their liberation would be all that is necessary to reform and moralize the State and convert it into a docile and disinterested instrument for the service of society.

Hence one must be staunch for republicanism, for in no more effective way could the State be returned to what in pure authoritarianism George conceived to be its original intention and function. This return could best be brought about and made secure by the collective motion of the average, the mass, acting in the political freedom which follows upon economic freedom. The logic of all this is sounder than its premises, for it is by no means probable that a new-found political liberty would be exercised in that way; indeed, if the expectations thus put upon the powers and disposition of the average be found excessive, it certainly would not be so exercised. But furthermore, as things stand, faith in republicanism is at the most no more than "the substance of things hoped for, the evidence of things not seen," because a true republic does not exist nor has ever existed. Hence to speak lightly of a republic and republican institutions as if they did exist anywhere outside of dreamland, is to make an unwarranted and culpable assumption—as for example, when George in a public address told his hearers that "republican government is yet but an experiment." Almost a hundred years before George made that speech, the superb scholarship and sterling honesty of John Adams had made it plain that the political organization of 1789 was not on a republican, but on an imperial model; it was but "a monarchical republic, or if you will, a limited monarchy," for the powers of the executive were far greater than those of "an avoyer, a consul, a podestá, a doge, a stadtholder; nay, than a king of Poland; nay, than a king of Sparta." It was but the kind of republic which Guizot said scornfully "begins with Plato, and necessarily ends with a policeman." If this were true in 1789—and it was true—what was to be said of it in George's day, after a century of continuous centralization and consolidation? But George did not need the scholarship of Adams to make him aware that republicanism was unrealized, nay, even unapproached; he had only to apply his reflective power to what he saw—to what, in

An Essay

fact, he had himself described in the clearest of terms. Murdstone's masterpiece of political inventiveness, the party-system, whereby "the people are simply permitted to choose which gang shall plunder them"—was this a republican institution?

George's ideas on the general subject of government and the State were never clear nor did he ever attempt to clarify them. When he dealt with the subject in writing, he was superficial, inconsistent, sometimes by implication self-contradictory. He had occasional revulsions, but they never got him anywhere. In 1881 he wrote a friend, "Yes, look at the Republican party, and also look at the Democratic party. It is pot and kettle. I am done." Done he might have been with those parties for the time being, though even so, he was not actually done with the Democratic party. Done with the party-system he never was, nor with the principle of party-organization. At no time would his notion of finding an appropriate vehicle for carrying forward his reforms have risen above the utter ineptitude of constructing another political party.

Thus such ideas as he had in this order were essentially indistinguishable from those current around him. He was sure that the State could be moralized only if and when the average man were moralized, and in this he was right. He was equally hopeful that the average man would moralize himself adequately, and would competently bring his moralization to bear on public affairs, as soon as his state of freedom—economic, political and social—had liberated his natural capacity and permitted his natural disposition freely to assert itself; and here he was walking on extremely treacherous ground. There was very possibly a far deeper insight expressed in a chance remark of the French painter Horace Vernet than appears in all George's presumptions upon human character. *"A la bonne heure,"* Vernet said with a gay irony, "give me a republic such as we understand it in France, all rulers, all natural-born kings, gods in mortals' disguise who dance to the piping of the devil. There have been two such since I was born; there may be another half-dozen like them within the next two centuries, because before you can have an ideal republic you must have ideal republicans, and nature can not afford to fool away her most precious gifts on a lot of jackleg lawyers and hobnail-booted riffraff. She condescends now and then to make an ideal tyrant, but she will never make a nation of ideal republicans; you may quite as well ask her to make a nation of Raphaels, Michelangelos, Shakespeares or Molières."

IV

On being summarily relieved from duty as a campaign speaker, George knocked about New York through the rest of the summer, writing a friend that "I don't know precisely what I shall do," but at the same time saying that he was no Micawber, but would find something to work at, even if he had to go back to typesetting. In the autumn, by an odd coincidence, he got a job at devilling for Abram S. Hewitt, who was to defeat him six years later as a candidate for the mayoralty of New York. Hewitt was then a member of Congress, and had to write a report on a subject which was apparently in some way too much for him, so he hired George at fifty dollars a week to get it into shape. This kept George going very well for four months; and meanwhile *Progress and Poverty* was rubbing along, holding its own, or a little better, but in no respect behaving like an epoch-maker. It might have gone on so indefinitely, until its limited market was saturated, and in default of a miracle it would have done so if a remarkable and most interesting event had not taken place. From the short-time point of view of the publicist, propagandist, crusader, this event was the best thing that could conceivably have happened; from the long-time point of view of the philosopher, it was the very worst imaginable. That event was the publication of a small work, hardly more than a tract, which George wrote at odd times while he was engaged on getting up Hewitt's report. Its title was *The Irish Land Question.*

This was a mere piece of pamphleteering, like his previous work on California's land-policy, but much better; it took rank at once with *Common Sense* and *The Rights of Man.* It merely generalized the Irish question in the simplest way, showing the situation there to be in all respects essentially the same as in England, America, or wherever the like system of private rent-monopoly prevails. Hence it affords probably the best general introduction to George's philosophy. If one were advising a student, one would suggest that he begin by reading this pamphlet, following it with *Protection or Free Trade,* and following that with *Progress and*

An Essay

Poverty; for reversing this order, as is commonly done, makes difficulties which are easily avoidable.

Curiously, the simple-hearted man wrote this pamphlet with no notion whatever of the effect it would have on his personal fortunes. Irish landlordism was at the moment the most conspicuous public question before the English-speaking world, everybody was talking about it, it was a first-class "horrible example" to put before economic dipsomaniacs; well, there it was, apparently made to order for someone to pick up and use for driving home the central truth set forth at large in *Progress and Poverty*—why not do that? So George did it as simply so much in the day's work; and the next thing he knew, a prodigious rabble of charmed and enthusiastic Irish had hoisted him on their shoulders and borne him into world-wide fame. Irish-like, their enthusiasm and loyalty were personal, unreasoning, unquestioning, and all the stronger for that. They were unimpressed by George as a philosopher, they did not care a Sassenach sixpence for his generalizations or his logic. All they cared about was that he was notably and powerfully "agin the government";

he was all on their side, and all against the rapacious and accursed landlords.

From that moment George, the reformer, crusader, the protagonist of a "movement," was a made man. The bolted doors of opportunity opened to him of their own accord. In New York City his market-value went up like a skyrocket. Lecturing went up; writing went up; and most significantly, sales of the moribund *Progress and Poverty* doubled, redoubled and doubled again to proportions which assured it of becoming a world's best seller. Nothing could stop it, with Irish affairs in the state they were, and with America's metropolis bung-full of immigrant politically-minded Irishmen who had come over in a steady stream for years as involuntary industrial exiles. One would give anything for a racial census of *Progress and Poverty's* purchasers in New York City during the years 1881-1882.

The uprising against landlordism in Ireland had reached the stage of undeclared war; there was every evidence that it would last a long time and grow much worse before the issue was settled. The British State, headed by Gladstone, had been policing Ireland with a military constabulary of 15,000, and a force of 40,000 from the regular army. As matters grew worse, the British State went on from one coercive measure to another, jailing Parnell, Dillon, Davitt, O'Kelly, with some hundreds of subordinate insurrectionists; suppressing the Land League; suspending the *habeas corpus;* searching and seizing without warrant—it governed sheerly as a ruthless and vindictive military despotism, until resistance was broken and a compromise patched up in the summer of 1882.

While George was still in California, hopefully perusing the first straggling reviews of *Progress and Poverty* early in 1880, Parnell and Dillon had come over under the auspices of the most influential Irish newspaper in New York, the *Irish World,* and made a tour of the country, stirring up a deal of enthusiasm and collecting almost a quarter-million dollars to carry on the war. It was an irregular proceeding, but as the American Irish had a great many votes and a very decent notion of how to use them, the government hardly saw its way to do anything about it. In the autumn of 1880, when George was in New York, Davitt came over to keep the fires burning. George met him, gave him a copy of *Progress and Poverty,* telling him it was distinctly down his street, and asked him to push it in England, which Davitt promised to do. George no doubt had a newspaper-reader's knowledge of the Irish fracas, but this meeting gave him his only first-hand acquaintance with the state of things there. The upshot of it was his pamphlet on the *Irish Land Question;* the upshot of the pamphlet was an overnight thrust into international fame—reprints of it came out at once in London, Manchester and Glasgow—and the upshot of fame was an offer to go over to the seat of war as a special correspondent of the *Irish World,* at sixty dollars a week and expenses. George proposed taking his wife and two daughters with him, but had not enough money to take himself over, let alone a family. Hearing of this in some way, however, and knowing George to be always in straits, a well-to-do man who had already placed a thousand copies of *Progress and Poverty* in public libraries throughout the country, came forward with money enough to clear some of George's most pressing debts and send the family-party off; and so they went.

George had arranged with the *Irish World* to stay three months, but instead he stayed a year, almost to the day; he sailed from New York on the fifteenth of October, 1881, and

An Essay

from Queenstown, on his return voyage, the fourth of October, 1882. It is not necessary to give a complete journal of his activities during the year in the British Isles; a light sketch of them will suffice. The thing to be remarked is that on leaving New York he laid aside the philosopher's robe, practically for good and all. Putting it vulgarly, he checked his whole philosophical equipment into storage late in 1881, and did not call for it again for four years; then he got it out for use while writing his *Protection or Free Trade.* Then he rechecked it, taking it out once more in 1891 for his *Science of Political Economy,* which his death left incomplete. Thus the course of his life from the autumn of 1881 to his death in the autumn of 1897, is one which those who have correctly appraised his superlative qualities of mind must follow with profound and unrelieved regret.

6

GEORGE'S ship touched at Cobh, which then bore the name of Queenstown, and he got off there, though his original intention had been to keep on to Liverpool; he was impatient to get into the thick of things. The Land Leaguers had advance-notice of him through the *Irish World;* and this, combined with his reputation as author of his pamphlet, insured him a rousing welcome to Dublin, whither he went as fast as a train would take him. The first thing in order was the inevitable public speech; four committees promptly waited on him to demand it. The crowd made a great demonstration after his address, attempting to unhitch his cab-horse and drag him homeward through the streets in a sort of triumphal procession. Not knowing the custom, George keenly resented this attention as "undemocratic," which is hardly the word that an informed person would apply in the premises; his use of it shows somewhat, perhaps, how fixed, isolated and mechanical his conception of democracy was. After this send-off he devoted some days to discharging his duties as a correspondent, making acquaintances, learning his way around in the Irish end of the imbroglio; and then he crossed to London to see what the British end of it was like.

His frame of mind on approaching Ireland was not judicial. Two weeks after leaving the ship, he wrote from Dublin that "I got indignant as soon as I landed, and I have not got over it yet. This is the most damnable government that exists today out of Russia; Miss Helen Taylor says, outside of Turkey." At that time, certainly, the British State was quite open to this charge, as it was in Mr. Jefferson's time, when he declared it to be "the most flagitious which has existed since the days of Philip of Macedon." Yet George might well have asked himself, and so might Mr. Jefferson, whether the British State was not acting pretty strictly in character as a State—whether the French State, the German State, the American State or any other State, would not have behaved quite as damnably if placed in the same circumstances. Here again one sees an occasion which should have moved him to examine the State as an institution; to trace its history as far back as possible, and consider how the institution originated, and why, and what its invariable primary intention, purpose and function have always been and now are, wherever the State exists. If he had done this, as he might have done if he had kept strictly to his character as a philosopher, it would have brought about some highly important modifications in his work. One would say that a thoughtful perusal of Spencer's *Social Statics* could not well have helped stirring his intellectual curiosity and turning it in this direction; but here, apparently, his bad habit of, as he called it, reading "at" a book, instead of reading it, stood in his way. It would almost appear that he never read anything in *Social Statics* except the brief passage which he cites in *Progress and Poverty;* this being the famous ninth chapter, which expounds "the right to the use of the earth," and which in 1892 Spencer indirectly repudiated.

George had not been many days in Ireland without having it borne in on him that politics, politicians and political organizations in that unhappy country were exactly what they are elsewhere. At the end of a month he wrote that there was a great deal of shillyshallying in the

An Essay

Land League movement, "more than I thought before coming here; and I think this is especially true of the leaders." He was disagreeably surprised to find that "with very many of those for whom it is doing the most, the *Irish World* is anything but popular; and I have felt from the beginning as if there was a good deal of that feeling about myself." Naturally so; like Strafford in 1633, George and the *Irish World* were for a policy of "Thorough" in dealing with Irish affairs; they were for pushing passive resistance to a finish without compromise, and for sustaining their policy by a campaign of intensive education. In short, they were for principle. The Irish politicians, on the other hand, being politicians, were for only so much principle as could be manœuvred into consistency with a general policy of opportunism. Hence, as George wrote Patrick Ford, the editor of the *Irish World,* "we are regarded as dangerous allies."

This feeling grew in step with the growth of George's popularity. George was inclined at first, and perhaps throughout, to attribute it to jealousy. In one of his early letters to Ford, he wrote that "sometimes it seems to me as if a lot of small men had found themselves in the lead of a tremendous movement, and finding themselves lifted into importance and power they never dreamed of, are jealous of anybody else sharing the honour." There may have been something in this, but as far as the principal men in the movement were concerned—Parnell, Davitt, Healy, Brennan, O'Kelly, Egan, Dillon —it is highly improbable that there was anything in it; indeed, George specifically exempted Parnell and Davitt from the suspicion of jealousy. The fact is that nothing throws a politician into such an agony of nervous horror as the idea of enforced association with a man of principle; a man to whom expediency means nothing, to whom opportunism is contemptible and compromise is utterly loathsome; and confidential association with George presented precisely this harrowing difficulty.

The Irish leaders smelt this breed of rat in George at the outset; his pamphlet exuded a rank unmistakable stench of it from every page; and when he arrived he found them ready for him. They were polite and pleasant; in fact, they were extremely cordial when circumstances threw him in their company, but they sought no such occasions, and when he brought up the subject of landlordism and the League movement, they never had anything to say. They treated him to a fine exhibition of that peculiarly seductive indirection and mendacity wherein the cultivated Irishman is so exquisitely accomplished. As time went on, George made it clearer and clearer to the Irish public that he and the politicians were not after the same thing; their views and aims were not his. To them, the Anglo-Irish economic war was an end-in-itself; to him, it was the preliminary skirmish in a world-wide revolutionary struggle. Hence as George's popularity grew, and the disparity of purpose became more and more manifest, the greater grew their uneasiness and apprehension lest this cosmopolitan politician, as latterly some of them called him, should steal their show.

After the murder of the Chief Secretary and his associate in Phœnix Park, on the sixth of May, 1882, the "movement" fizzled out precisely as from the beginning any competent observer of politics, politicians and political methods might have known it would. It ended in one of those compromises which are knaved up out of the obscene freemasonry existing among politicians of all schools and parties, whereby opponents who roundly abuse each other in public for electioneering purposes, quietly meet in private and talk turkey, with one eye closed. Parnell and Gladstone got together; they were the late Theodore Roosevelt's kind of "practical men." Thereafter George was an excommunicate outcast; even Davitt, the one man who had some sympathetic understanding of what George was driving at, became very fidgety about being seen in his company, and avoided him when he could decently do so.

II

In Ireland, George thought of himself first and last as a combatant. He wrote Ford that "my sympathies are so strongly with this fight against such tremendous odds of every kind, that it is impossible for me not to feel myself in it." In his own eyes he was not a disinterested observer and reporter, but another Lafayette of old, bent on breaking the bondage of tyranny and oppression which lay so heavy upon the Irish people. In this capacity he committed acts which were thoroughly inconsistent with his actual status as an alien journalist visiting Ireland on sufferance—in theory, a guest of the British State—and therefore under an implied

An Essay

commitment to abstain from seditious practices. In strict justice, he should have received a severe lesson in the proprieties, but Mr. Gladstone had strong reasons for keeping as far as possible on the blind side of Uncle Sam at the moment—the American State was under heavy pressure from the mass of Irish-American voting-power, and might at any time give way if its susceptibilities were not very carefully managed—so George's activities were not too closely looked into. Twice, indeed, he was arrested and jailed in Ireland, subjected to search, and brought before a local magistrate; but nothing incriminating was found in his possession, and he was released under a sort of Scotch verdict of "not guilty, but don't do it again." One may be of two minds about George's behaviour; certainly it was such as only an enthusiast strongly tinctured with fanaticism would normally exhibit, and no doubt the thought never once crossed his mind that it might be questionable. Whatever the motives of Mr. Gladstone and his associates may have been, they showed great forbearance with George, and so did a considerable section of British society which privately must have regarded him as a most insensitive person and a distressing annoyance.

One who has any acquaintance with England and its ways may see a great deal of humour and no less pathos in the account of George's first visit to London, whither he went from Ireland after a month or so, to carry the war into the enemy's country. Some few who were prominent in British literary and political society were also prominent sympathizers with the Irish movement; George had already met two or three of them in Dublin. These took him up, inviting him here and there in the regular way, to gatherings where seasoned persons of vast experience, daily and hourly in contact with all sorts and conditions of men, might meet him and look him over. One wonders mightily what they made of him. Those who were sensitive to such impressions, such as Bright, Joseph Chamberlain, Walter Besant, must have been struck by the essential goodness which pervaded his presence, his noble single-mindedness and simplicity of heart; and were all the more puzzled, no doubt, to find a way of reconciling this with other qualities which by all accounts he possessed, and indeed gave evidence of possessing. His status in the Irish affair seemed unnatural, anomalous; a Francis doubled by a Spinoza and fused into a Peter the Hermit was something they were not prepared for; there must be an out about it somewhere. Decidedly the man was an enigma, but he came out of that extraordinary American civilization which seemed to be a breeding-ground of odd monstrosities—one might best perhaps let him go at that for the moment, and see what comes of him.

Others, like Browning and Tennyson, looked on him without interest and passed him by; he did not meet them, though once, at least, they were in the same company throughout an evening. He set great store by the prospect of meeting Herbert Spencer, but when the ailing and crabbed old bachelor-philosopher had with great toil and vexation dragged himself out to an evening party, and the chance came, George was grievously disappointed. The ninth chapter of *Social Statics* had prepared him to find Spencer red-hot on the Irish side, but the old man was not; perhaps out of indifference, perhaps out of sheer perversity, he gave George to understand that he was aggressively on the side of the landlords. They had but few words together, and parted on terms of imperishable dislike and distrust. It is clear from a passage in one of Spencer's later essays in which he makes George out to be a collectivist, that he never read George's work, for George was one of the most formidable anti-collectivists, as well as the most radical, who ever lived. His work leaves not a shred of plausibility attaching to any of the Protean forms of collectivism now rampant in the world, whether Marxist, Hitlerian, "totalitarian," Fabian, "Christian," or what-you-will; and here he was completely at one with Spencer. He did, unfortunately, advocate the State-socialization of economic rent, as Spencer himself had done in *Social Statics;* it is the only weak spot in George's social scheme, easily amended and therefore unimportant. The only point that a critic ever scored off George was made by the Duke of Argyll on the head of this one weakness. George's closest approach to anything savouring of collectivism, however, was in this advocacy of a national, rather than a local, confiscation of rent; and this was not close enough to be disturbing.

The feud that smouldered between George and Spencer was by no means creditable to either, but it was so amusing in its naïveté and pettiness that one could not take it seriously or regard it as anything but a diverting display of two great men in motley. George thought

Spencer was the victim of a corroding vanity; shortly after their little passage-at-arms he wrote an American friend to "discount Herbert Spencer. He is most horribly conceited, and I don't believe really great men are." George did not have enough of the saving grace of humour to perceive that, on the evidence offered, it would have been perfectly competent for Spencer to think the same thing of him. In Spencer's view, a pernicious foreigner starring it around the country, stirring up the wretched Irish to a fever of treasonable turbulence, and generally laying down the law on matters of purely municipal administration—"a man with a mission," as the *Standard* ironically said, "born to set right in a single generation the errors of six thousand years"—why, to describe such a man as horribly conceited would be the next thing to a compliment.

George held to this view of Spencer throughout. When Spencer made an indirect revocation of the principle which he had laid down forty years before in the ninth chapter of *Social Statics*, George again wrote the same friend that "Spencer is going the way of Comte; going insane from vanity." George promptly attacked Spencer for his supposititious apostasy, in a sizable pamphlet which provoked a considerable discussion in England, involving persons of prominence in both public life and academic life. Spencer made no direct reply, but he incited his friends to action, denouncing George to them with bitter vehemence. It was a sorry affair on both sides. As a matter of controversy, George had all the best of it; taking his arguments out of Spencer's own mouth, he had an easy victory, so easy that he might have gone to any length of urbanity and amenity without losing ground. His pamphlet was a superb masterpiece of polemics, but almost equally conspicuous for its bad taste and its utter failure in generosity; its flat assertion of interested motives on Spencer's part was wholly gratuitous, wholly devoid of foundation, and as unkind as it was uncalled-for. It at once pitched George's side of the controversy on a plane so low that no self-respecting person could bring himself to meet it. To disqualify Spencer as a sycophant to British landlords, "a fawning Vicar of Bray, clothing in pompous phraseology and arrogant assumption logical confusions so absurd as to be comical"—there is but one word to be applied to an imputation of motive such as this; it is scurrilous.

An Essay

The whole episode is simply so much clear evidence of the supreme silliness of making a system of philosophy the subject-matter of public controversy or a campaign of propaganda. After all, now that the acerbities of debate have been long forgotten and the debaters have long since taken their places in literary history, the two great works still stand untouched; no spate of cavil, prepossession or personal disharmony affects them. The earth moved around the sun as regularly after Galileo's recantation as it did before. The validity of *Social Statics* and of *Progress and Poverty* would remain unimpaired today if their authors had disavowed every line of them. They are, taken together, the complete formulation of the philosophy of human freedom; the one complements the other. Nothing substantial has ever been said against either of them; nothing can be said. Anyone may examine them and make up his own mind about their validity. If and when the moral and intellectual capacities of average humanity permit their general acceptance, they will be generally accepted; and as Homenas said of the Decretals, "no sooner than then, nor otherwise than thus" shall their theory be translated into fruitful practice. Meanwhile, obviously, those capacities being what they are, any attempt to urge upon the masses of mankind an acceptance of a social theory which they are unable to accept and still less able to assimilate, is to the last degree futile and mischievous.

George resented this limitation with all the force of his ardent humanitarianism, and his career as a propagandist was a continuous course of impassioned, reckless, almost hysterical kicking against its pricks. Spencer's evolutionary doctrine, which he never in the least understood, awoke in him a passion of the *odium theologicum* which would have delighted the heart of his old fundamentalist shepherd, the Rev. Josiah Jupp. In 1880, before the publication of *Progress and Poverty,* he mentions in a letter his desire sometime to write "a dissection of this materialistic philosophy which, with its false assumption of science, passes current with so many." Happily, his friends dissuaded him from this project, telling him frankly that he was not equal to it; he had neither undergone the discipline, nor possessed the information, necessary for such a task. His terms "materialistic" and "the false assumption of science" come straight out of the standard ecclesiastical glossary—one might even go so far

An Essay

as to say, out of the standard ecclesiastical cant. The Rev. Josiah Jupp could pretty well have got copyright on them. One may quite see how George's view of man's psychical constitution as now existing—the view reflected in *Progress and Poverty*—must have seemed, not to the doctrinaire materialist and mechanist, not to evolutionists like Darwin, Wallace, Youmans, Spencer, but to the strong common sense of a moderate and agnostic Huxley, for example, who said in a letter to Knowles that "it is more damneder nonsense than poor Rousseau's blether." George, however, maintained this view to the end, and in the end gave his life for it: a nobler sacrifice was never made, nor a more ill-judged one.

Spencer was, in fact, as sound a humanitarian as George; he insisted, however, that philanthropic activity should be based on the consideration of ultimate good rather than proximate good. Experience has shown beyond peradventure that his criticism of State activity, taking shape in what we now call "social legislation," is abundantly sound. "In our days of active philanthropy," he says in a postscript to his essays on *The Man Versus the State,* "hosts of people eager to achieve benefits for their less fortunate fellows by what seem the shortest methods, are busily occupied in developing administrative arrangements proper to a lower type of society; are bringing about retrogression while aiming at progression. The normal difficulties in the way of advance are sufficiently great, and it is lamentable that they should be made greater. Hence," he added, with reference to his essays, "something well worth doing may be done if philanthropists can be shown that they are in many cases insuring the future ill-being of men while eagerly pursuing their present well-being."

Spencer also, like George, believed that the moral and intellectual constitution of mankind is indefinitely improvable; and again like George, he was an optimist in regard to this improvement. He based both his belief and his optimism, however, on the postulate of indefinite time, which George did not. The postscript above mentioned shows that he had no illusions about the degree to which that improvement had already advanced, and therein he differed from George; but his optimism remained to guide him to a sound conclusion in respect of the function of a social philosopher in the circumstances. However low the degree of development in the individual and in society, it remains true that—

an ideal, far in advance of practicability though it may be, is always needful for right guidance. If, amid all those compromises which the circumstances of the times necessitate, or are thought to necessitate, there exist no true conceptions of better and worse in social organizations; if nothing beyond the exigencies of the moment are attended to, and the proximately-best is habitually identified with the ultimately-best; there cannot be any true progress. However distant may be the goal, and however often intervening obstacles may necessitate deviation in our course towards it, it is obviously requisite to know whereabouts it lies.

It was impossible for George to reconcile himself to this conclusion; to agree that at the present time, and with the average man's psychical development at its present extremely low level, it is the sole business of the humanitarian and optimistic philosopher to establish those true conceptions, to disengage and exhibit the ultimately-best, to show clearly whereabouts the goal of society lies, and leave the result to be what it may. Yet clearly one may see how far this conclusion is from inducing the "fatalism" which George erroneously attributed to Spencer and his disciples; or from fostering either a Laodicean or a Corinthian type of cultivated inaction. It merely deprecates and disallows action which, however appropriate to conditions as yet non-existent, is distinctly inappropriate to conditions actually existing; and it reminds us that a course of such anticipatory action is bound to end in so worsening existing conditions as to put a realization of the anticipated conditions much further off than it would otherwise be. It counsels inaction where in the nature of things even right action—right, that is, in reference to another set of circumstances than those existing—is inadmissible; and the wisdom of this counsel is invariably justified in the outcome.

III

Most conspicuously was it justified in the case of George's campaign of propaganda in the British Isles. When the bottom dropped out of the Irish Land League movement, George turned to the idea of pushing *Progress and Poverty* in England. He put in most of the year 1882 at this, so satisfactorily that after a year's stay in America he returned there in 1883 for another visit which amounted to a protracted tour of lecturing and organizing, lasting somewhat over three months.

His first visit made him better known in England than in America, as was shown by a most amusing and significant incident. When he came back to New York in October, 1882, he found himself quite the man of the hour. The American Irish were in a state of frantic disgust with the Parnell-Gladstone compromise; they had given up a good deal of money and interest for a policy of "Thorough," and when the movement ended in an inglorious fiasco, they felt, not without reason, that they had been betrayed and bilked. The breeze raised in the United States against the partition of Czechoslovakia was a mild zephyr by comparison with the hurricane raised by Irish agitation against the treaty of Kilmainham. Naturally, then, Irish-American appreciation of George as the great apostle and prophet of "Thorough," the one who had manfully stood on the burning deck whence all but him had fled, rose to still greater heights. When his ship came in, the whole sum-total of Irish-led organization in New York City was on hand, electrified with the robust vivacity which Irish enterprise puts into such demonstrations. To get an idea of the impressiveness of all this, it must be remembered that in those days the whole political organization of the city, and most of its politico-social and politico-economic organization as well, was Irish-led; and that this leadership also commanded the usual numerous retinue of non-Irish hangers-on who followed it for the promotion of their own purposes. So George, finding himself, as he naïvely said, "pretty near famous," was met not only by Irish enthusiasts, but also by uproarious crowds of miscellaneous gentry out of all peoples, nations and languages —Parthians, Medes and Elamites, Jews, Turks, infidels and heretics—all set to do him honour, and withal to show what the American Irish thought of the infamous Kilmainham treaty.

Of all the city's institutions, perhaps the most solidly Irish were the bench and bar; even more solidly Irish then than they are Jewish now. They combined with representative trade and commerce to give George a complimentary dinner at Delmonico's; ten dollars a plate, *vin non compris!* The guests represented everything that was influential, distinguished, accomplished. Hon. Algernon S. Sullivan presided. Rev. Henry Ward Beecher spoke; so did Judge van Brunt, Judge Arnoux, Francis B.

An Essay 161

Thurber, and others as prominent. In the simplicity of his heart, when George entered the room and laid eyes on all this array of gorgeousness, he whispered to one of the steering-committee, "How did you ever get them to come?" Really, one must wonder how far *Progress and Poverty* could have got in New York where it had been bought at a great rate for a year, since none of these dignitaries seemed to have the faintest idea of who George was, or what he was, but took him for an Irishman, an Irish patriot who had twice been sloughed up in jail as a British prisoner! Even the newspapers which reported the event at considerable length next morning seemed, with but one exception, as ill-informed. One of George's friends, Mr. Louis F. Post, tells the story that after the dinner at Delmonico's, Recorder Smythe caught him by the arm and asked, "What part of Ireland does this man George come from?"

"He isn't an Irishman," Mr. Post replied. "He was born in Philadelphia, and so was his father before him."

The Recorder looked puzzled, and presently murmured, half to himself and half to Mr. Post, "No-o-o, that can hardly be; I was told that he was born in Ireland."

No such misapprehensions existed in England. Leading men among the British had a good sound idea of what George was, and in general they took him for what he was. In general, moreover, to their credit be it said, their idea was a fair idea, and their play with him was fair play. Dislike the British as one may, distrust them in their collective capacity as one should, one must with profound respect perceive in their treatment of George a notable instance of "the ancient and inbred integrity, piety, good nature, and good humour, of the people of England"—a characterization which was made, not by one of their own, but by an Irishman, Edmund Burke; and which still remains the truest characterization ever made of that people. There were exceptions in the case of eminent individuals; Spencer was one. Those who took up the cudgels against him often misunderstood both the substance and the incidence of his contentions; Bright did, and so did the Duke of Argyll, Chamberlain, Fawcett, Toynbee, Frederic Harrison, Conybeare. Nor is this to be wondered at when one considers that he appeared before the country as primarily a political proletarian agitator; the only gifts and methods which he put on display were those of the popular orator, organizer, demagogue. One can only wonder, not that the philosopher was sometimes confused with the spellbinder, but that in the circumstances the distinction between them should ever have been drawn.

Yet drawn it was, and on the whole, quite fairly and carefully drawn, considering that George's public activities so little suggested that it should be drawn, and so strongly suggested that it should not. As a rule, speaking in the phrase of sport, George got a run for his money in England; his intellectual respectability was recognized and appreciated by representative Englishmen—distinctly so, by comparison with the persistent incomprehension and depreciation visited on it by his own countrymen. He was regarded as a serious person, a man of parts, to be dealt with seriously; not to be snubbed, vilified into obscurity, or victimized by a conspiracy of silence. He and his doctrines got, in short, as fair treatment as could reasonably be asked for them, and fairer treatment than a disinterested view of his self-chosen public character would lead one to expect.

IV

George's plans for circulating *Progress and Poverty* in England were well laid. Unlike Americans, the British public has long been accustomed to paying for political pamphlets and reading them carefully; hence this form of literature is much better prepared and more highly developed there than here where campaign-documents are given away by the cartload and mostly go unread. As a first step, George bought from the Glasgow publishers a set of plates of his pamphlet on the Irish land question, and got out an edition of five thousand, to be sold at threepence (six cents, American money); thinking quite rightly that nothing could better stimulate a popular demand for *Progress and Poverty*. He also arranged for a new imprint of the latter book in the form of an overgrown pamphlet, eighty-eight pages quarto, at twelve cents. The initial expense of this pamphleteering project was met by a gift from a friend in America, which George acknowledged by saying hopefully, "Now we shall start the revolution!"

The book went like wildfire with a speed

that was extraordinary, even considering that the regular edition had done astonishingly well. More than forty thousand copies of the cheap edition were sold in the first year, and naturally the effects were felt throughout the Empire; one house in Melbourne sent in an initial order for thirteen hundred copies. Sales were promoted in the customary ways, by the distribution of samples, circularizing, advertising in the newspapers, although the book was going ahead so fast under its own steam that there seems to have been no need of this pressure. The *Times,* that imposing organ of the Empire's financial and commercial interests, gave it a five-column review, treating it respectfully, ceremoniously and favourably; and this piece of complaisance from the old "Thunderer" set the fashion for other British publications. Meanwhile George was busily lecturing, debating, organizing, forgathering with religionists, humanitarians, philanthropists, doing anything and everything, as he was fond of saying, to "spread the Light." Like his great prototype on the shores of the Mediterranean, he had early in the game—much earlier than St. Paul did—given up hope of the orthodox children of the Covenant. After three months of looking over the situation, he wrote, "I have little hope of the literary class here—never at all of the men who have made their reputations. It is the masses whom we must try to educate." *Ecce convertimur ad gentes!*—and to this task he applied himself so vigorously that when he left the country he was, with the possible exception of Mr. Gladstone, the most talked-of man in England.

All this took place in 1882, during his first visit, while his status was nominally still that of correspondent for the *Irish World*. After his departure, his influence and prestige grew even faster. *Progress and Poverty* went on selling and being read; Englishmen really read it. The disciples which George had made in England, the organizations he had fostered, pushed the "movement" to even greater prosperity all over the Empire; George became as familiarly and favourably known in the antipodes as he was in Manchester and Glasgow. All kinds of offers came his way. He had an offer of backing to start a paper in London, a proposal to change his citizenship and become a British subject, proposals to write for British periodicals, and he was offered a choice of three or four constituencies in which to run as a candidate for membership in the House of Commons. Finally it was proposed that the least he could do would be to make a second missionary journey through England and Scotland; and this he did.

On this whirlwind tour of incessant propaganda-work, he had two main objects in view. The first was to make unmistakably clear his attitude towards all the works and ways of collectivism. He did this in so aggressive and workmanlike a style that one wonders anew at Spencer's ludicrous error in classing him with the collectivists. He preached straight individualism by day and by night, in and out of season. On the Marxians led by the brilliant and able Hyndman, he declared open war, no quarter, and no prisoners taken. Socialists and near-socialists of whatever breed or brand went into debate with him only to die a horrible death under torture of the rack and thumbscrew. Never was he worsted, never forced to a tactical retreat. Never had the world seen such a powerful popular exponent of uncompromising individualism, nor has it seen another like him since his day.

His second object was to make clear his policy of "Thorough" in respect of the confiscation of economic rent. There were a good many middle-of-the-road men in England who were prepared to go part-way with George, indeed who would be glad, some of them, to go all the way with him; but who thought that since the policy of "Thorough" was quite impracticable, half a loaf would be better than no bread. In principle, they would have readily subscribed to Spencer's statement that "the right of mankind-at-large to the earth's surface is still valid; all deeds, customs and laws notwithstanding"; yet they thought that for prudential reasons it was injudicious to avow this statement, with its obvious corollaries and implications, as a practical working-policy. At the same time, they were against the socialists' proposal to have the State take over the land and manage it directly; they were as yet a little too far gone in British tradition to get down such an unprecedented dose of Statism without gagging. Hence they took refuge in various characteristically "liberal" milk-and-bilgewater compromise-measures which aimed at placating everyone without satisfying anyone; such, for instance, as the eminent Alfred Russell Wallace's proposal that the State should buy out the landlords, and then farm out the land to actual users under a system of annual quit-rent.

George was down on all this sort of dillydallying, hammer and tongs. Again a simon-pure Spencerian, he was for "Thorough." He was for it undiluted, unadulterated, unscented; he was for it with no paltering, no extenuation, and world without end. He went through England and Scotland, breathing out threatenings and slaughter indiscriminately against the proposals of collectivism and against the wishy-washy suggestions of "liberal" opportunism. The land belonged to the whole people, or it belonged to the landlords. If the latter, either set of proposals was iniquitous, and so was his own. No interference with the landlords' rights of ownership was admissible. If the former, the landlords were usurpers, they should be treated as such, and the people should resume possession. Buying the landlords out, proposing any kind of compensation or recognizing any kind of vested right as established by prescription, was simply compounding a felony. Had not Spencer showered a devastating irony on the whole conception of prescriptive right? "How long does it take," he asked in 1850, "for what was originally a wrong to grow into a right? At what rate per annum do invalid claims become valid? If a title gets perfect in a thousand years, how much more than perfect will it be in two thousand years?" No; no buying off of landlords or compounding their claims. But as against the collectivists, who were proposing that the State should take over the land itself, and administer it through a bureaucracy—again, No. There were the weightiest objections to such an irrevocable wholesale concession to Statism. Preserve the principle of individualism intact—nay, fortify and brace it—by letting the landlords monopolize all the land they like, and do with it what they like, but confiscate every farthing of the economic rent of that land, twenty shillings in every pound on full market-valuation, one hundred cents in every dollar.

V

George's inspiring march of progress brought results beyond his utmost expectation. Circumstances favoured him, as also they favoured the collectivists. The two rival social schemes ran neck and neck in the race for popular suffrage. Conditions were bad in London, and as bad if not a trifle worse in the great industrial towns which William Cobbett, years before, had bluntly called *Hell-holes*. Discontent was great, not only among the proletariat, but among that numerous class out of which George himself had but lately risen; a class so miserably poor as to be ranked a grade below the proletarian level. Growing also was the sentiment that something must be done; the earlier apostles of "social reform," Fielding, Dickens, Ruskin, Kingsley, were coming into their own. Philanthropy had a foothold in all classes; it was powerfully stimulated by a great output of exhibitory publications which echoed "the bitter cry of outcast London." Journalistic enterprise of the muckraking order found profit in serving up vivid stories of the vice and crime directly attributable to submergence in an environment "compared with which the lair of a wild beast would be a comfortable and healthy spot." George's efforts contributed directly to the volume of discontent. He had said, "It is the masses whom we must try to educate," and it was towards the masses that his efforts were continuously bent. He steadily incited the masses, as Burke said, "to a better sense of their condition," and did it with such force and earnestness that the masses thronged him, heard him gladly, read his books; and from this acclaim he drew an illusory assurance of his exceeding great reward.

Looking back over a perspective of almost sixty years, and asking what actually was the net result of George's efforts to educate the masses, one must answer, Less than nothing. Not only was it that the outcome was purely negative as far as any practical or fruitful acceptance of George's philosophy was concerned, but the only positive effect of his propaganda was indirectly to strengthen the movement towards the collectivism which he abhorred. The British State responded to the popular demand for "social reform" as Prince de Bismarck did in Germany when he took the wind out of the sails of his socialists by lifting the most eligible items out of their programme and administering them himself as a State enterprise. "If something is not done quickly to meet the growing necessities of the case," Mr. Chamberlain said, "we may live to see theories as wild and methods as unjust as those suggested by the American economist adopted as the creed of no inconsiderable portion of the electorate."

So something was done. The British State saw here a capital chance to work "the old trick," as James Madison contemptuously called it, "of turning every contingency into a resource for accumulating force in the government." Every governmental measure of "social reform" meant more laws, more boards and bureaux, more coercions, controls, supervisions, surveillances, more taxes, and less freedom for the individual. In other words, it meant a progressive conversion of social power into State power, a progressive weakening and depletion of the social structure, a progressive strengthening and enlargement of the State's structure; and to bring this about was precisely the aim of the collectivists. George, by making himself a mouthpiece of proletarian discontent and at the same time persistently proclaiming his faith in political action, encouraged the whole body of "liberal" reformers to demand from the State ever more and more stringent, more inclusive and more highly particularized measures of coercive "social legislation"; and this in turn encouraged the collectivists in their designs for making a clean sweep of all social power by converting it at once into State power. That George himself should not have perceived this unmistakable tendency inherent in his own self-chosen, self-directed activities, is almost incredible. As the Duke of Argyll pointed out from the eloquent arraignment which George had made in *Progress and Poverty,* George knew as well as anyone the monstrously evil character of the American State; yet it was to this institution that he proposed to commit the collection of the prodigious revenue proceeding from a national confiscation of economic rent, and the administration of this revenue for social purposes! But extraordinary as it seems, George never made even the simplest generalization from his own observations in *Progress and Poverty,* and therefore his achievements in Britain played straight into the hands of the collectivists; their course led straight to Statism.

One must now see that the upshot of the general movement for "social reform" to which George so largely contributed, is precisely what Herbert Spencer forecast in his essay called *The Coming Slavery.* The economic upshot is that as in Rome at the end of the second century, British productive social power has now been so far converted into unproductive State power that there is not enough of it left to pay the State's bills. The moral upshot is that individualism is moribund in England, beyond hope of revival. Its philosophy is forgotten, unread and unknown, and the Englishman rests with what resignation he can summon, in precisely the condition of State-servitude which Spencer predicted for him.

Such is the great victory of British collectivism at the present time; such is the state of things in which Mr. Hyndman and his associates might well rejoice if they were here to see it; and the state of things most certainly ensuing might perhaps rejoice them even more. All that being as it is, there is an immense pathos in the unfailing note of assurance which runs throughout George's letters from England to friends in America. Hardly had he landed on Irish soil, when he wrote, "It is the beginning of the revolution, sure"; and again, a few days later, "In spite of everything, the *light* is spreading." At the end of his first visit, he wrote, "Sure as we live, we have kindled the fire in England, and there is no human power that can put it out." During his great tour in England, and afterwards to the day of his death, his confidence was unshaken. "The future is ours"; "The cause moves on, no matter who falls"; "Now the currents of the time are setting in our favour"; "All the new forces of our civilization are with us and for us"—so he wrote, and so he believed, to the end.

7

WITHIN the next five years, George made two more missionary excursions to England, one very brief, lasting only a couple of weeks, and followed closely by another which occupied three months. His activities were the same as before, and his experience was differentiated mostly by finding that his doctrines had enlisted the support of persons who were socially several cuts above those who had previously led in his meetings. He noted that those who now occupied the platform "to move the votes of thanks that are customary there on such occasions, were men who formerly would not have thought of being in such a place . . . the local notables, the file leaders—the active workers, as we here would say—of the Radical wing of the Liberal party." Even Mr. Chamberlain had decorously cast a sheep's eye at the principle of land-value taxation; Henry Labouchère and T. P. O'Connor had espoused it; and in a negative way it had been at least countenanced by the Lord Chief Justice of England.

George remarked this change of attitude and temper, but seemed not over-impressed by it, nor did he make it the occasion of a closer approach to persons of a more influential order; he apparently took it all as so much clear gain, more or less as lagniappe or "velvet," and went on with his enterprise of evangelizing the masses.

In 1890, the year after his last round of the British Isles, he went on a tour of New Zealand and Australia, where by that time he had come into great repute and urgent demand; his fiscal doctrine had gone a long way there. His wife, who was an Australian, went with him. He elected to go by way of San Francisco, the scene of their earlier life together. Coming back to California after ten years, bearing all the wreaths of laurel he had won in distant parts of the earth, he was received with a tremendous demonstration. Australia made so much of him that he remained there three months, during which he pretty well covered the country, speaking every day but one, and sometimes twice a day. He came back to New York by the long way around, eastward to India, thence up through the Red Sea and the Mediterranean, using the long sea-trip for recuperation after his exhausting campaign. He left the ship at Brindisi, and made the hurried land-journey which has already been mentioned in these pages, through Italy, Switzerland and France to London. He made two speeches, one in London and one in Glasgow—he had but a day or two before his ship sailed—and he then bade England farewell forever.

II

Out of his short span of fifty-eight years, George spent approximately three years abroad and fifty-five in America; yet the result of his missionary endeavours was more solid and lasting in foreign parts than in his native land. In 1897 the British economist J. A. Hobson said that George might be considered as having exercised a more directly formative and educative influence over English radicalism since 1882 than any other man; which is no doubt true, but since 1897 that influence has evaporated. In America he was not wholly in the proverbial case of a prophet without honour in his own country, for in the course he laid out for himself he got great honour of a sort; but the course being what it was, the honour was special, in-

An Essay

substantial and evanescent. Abroad, in the estimation of a considerable élite, the philosopher was fairly clearly marked off from the humanitarian, the philanthropist and the agitator, and was rated at somewhere near a proper value; while at home the character which entitles him to humanity's profound and permanent intellectual respect was overshadowed and lost to sight. So completely did it disappear under a mass of misunderstanding, ignorant misrepresentation, interested calumny and studied neglect—under the brute mass of what Ernest Renan so finely terms *le matérialisme vulgaire, la bassesse de l'homme intéressé*—that even the sympathetic memory of his self-immolation on the altar of his cause did not outlast his generation.

His procedure at home was the same which he employed abroad. His task was to "educate the masses" here as there; and in his belief that the masses are educable, his unshaken trust was in the old familiar methods of publicity, agitation, organization and political action. Never did he become aware that education is as much, even more, a matter of time as of anything else; that it is impossible to tell anybody anything unless, in a very real sense, he knows it already.

When he returned to New York in 1882 from his first visit to England, he at once repeated the experiment which had succeeded so well with British readers, by getting out a cheap paper-covered edition of his two books. At that time, before the United States went into an international-copyright agreement, Americans were quite accustomed to paper-bound books. Most people, probably, have heard of the "dime novel," the terror of anxious mothers, the ancestor of what we now know as Western pulps. Those advanced in years can remember also the excellent popular literature purveyed by the Franklin Square Library at forty cents, and by the Seaside Library and Lovell's Library at ten cents, twenty cents for "double numbers." These enterprises were hard on authors whose works were pirated without so much as a by-your-leave, but they did a great public service; they furnished many a child with the beginnings of a lasting love of literature. George got his pamphlet on the Irish land question into Lovell's Library at ten cents, and *Progress and Poverty* as a double number at twenty cents.

In 1883, George also helped to start an organization called the Free Soil Society; it had ambitious plans for branching out on a national scale, but it did not "take" particularly, and died young. This was the second in a meandering string of organizations which mushroomed up out of George's fiscal scheme—the first one was the Land Reform League of California, already mentioned in these pages—and which soon quietly gave up an exiguous existence. He lectured here and there, and wrote much for popular publications on the social problems of the day. Many opportunities of the kind were open to him, and he had an added motive for embracing them because, as ever, he was in great need of money. He was perhaps the only author who ever lived whose books sold by the million in his own lifetime without yielding him so much as a decent living—at this very time he wrote a friend that "I have now just twenty-five dollars in the world." The proprietor of the *North American Review,* which was then seeing its best days, proposed starting a weekly under George's editorship, but George declined the offer, thinking the time for that had not yet come. Both in speaking and writing, his work was polemic, propagandist, popular in tone, constant to George's invariable aim at "educating the masses."

All this naturally tended to associate him in

the public mind not with the interests of the masses, but with what the public mind conceived those interests to be. It tended to pose him as a class-conscious proletarian publicist, and one is obliged to say, not without reason. Despite his assertion that in the long-time view he was not for any class, but for the abolition of classes through applying a policy of fundamental justice to all classes alike, the immediate incidence of his aims and sympathies was so obvious as to encourage misapprehensions out of which an interested antagonism might make anything it liked.

One thing which greatly helped to establish this misapprehension of George as only a class-conscious proletarian gonfalonier, was the discovery that something very close to his fiscal proposals was in the platform of the Knights of Labour, and had been there for some time. This organization was the parent of the American Federation; its principles were more radical and far more intelligent than those of its offspring; its leader was a man of considerable ability, named Terence V. Powderly. One of the statements in its declaration of principles was that—

The land, including all the natural sources of wealth, is the heritage of all the people, and should not be subject to speculative traffic. Occupancy and use should be the only title to the possession of land. Taxes should be levied upon its full value for use, exclusive of improvements, and should be sufficient to take for the community all unearned increment.

This was sound Georgian doctrine, even to the policy of "Thorough" set forth in the last clause. In fact, the words "for the community" hint at a local confiscation of rent, rather than at the disadvantageous policy of national confiscation which George contemplated; so to that extent they improve on him. How this plank got into the platform seems now to be unknown; it had lain long as a dead letter. There it was, however, and the Irish rent-war galvanized it into life. Powderly was Irish by descent; he made friends with George, pushed the cheap edition of his books throughout the organization, which by 1883 had covered the country and was at the height of its power. George joined the order. He had been a labour-union man in California, he was still a unionist in spirit, and moreover, he was a natural-born joiner; the spirit of organization was part of every breath he drew. So quite without thought of expediency, he became a Knight of Labour; and thus circumstances combined with his natural predilections to edge him a little closer towards the apparent status of an Adullamite demagogue, a bell-wether of the disaffected.

III

Yet it was at this time that he began to consider taking his philosophical equipment out of storage for use on a new book, the one which finally came out two years later, called *Protection or Free Trade*. One might say, continuing the figure, that he went as far as to visit the warehouse two or three times, look his equipment over, test it out, and then put it away again, before actually taking it off the premises and setting it up for a job of steady work. In other words, he wrote a bit piecemeal on his book, interrupting his work on it several times with lectures, propagandist essays, a voyage to England, and a long reply to the Duke of Argyll's attack in the *Nineteenth Century*. George wanted to complete the book, meant to do it, and finally did it; but a sense of what he thought was his immediate and paramount duty

An Essay

to the "cause" persistently blocked his progress, so that a year elapsed with little to show.

He meant the book to be timely, and so it was, although the final turn of public affairs was not quite so favourable to it as he expected. The tariff-question was uppermost at the time, and George thought Cleveland's election in 1884 would force it to a clear issue, but it did not; for while Cleveland sent a message to Congress advocating a lower tariff, he also made it clear that he was by no means for free trade, not even for the principle of free trade. He was for "tariff reform," which represented no principle whatever—it could be made to mean anything that anybody chose to make it mean—and was therefore congenial to the influential self-styled liberal element throughout the country, led by such publicists as Sumner, Beecher, Curtis, Godkin; and it was naturally and necessarily congenial to politicians who had an ear to the ground. After years of observation and experience, George still cherished the infatuated belief that a politician is capable of publicly and formally recognizing a principle; he remained unaware of the simple truth that if a politician were thus capable, he would not only cease to be a politician, but would not, and could not, have become one in the first instance. Cleveland's message was a wet blanket on George, but he still had hopes of him on his second nomination in 1888; and when Cleveland was renominated and elected in 1892, George's hopes rose higher. Cleveland, however, suddenly shelved the tariff and made the currency the main issue on which his party took its stand. George was then through with Cleveland; he prophesied that in time to come, the philosophical historian would write of him "as more dangerous to the republic than any of his predecessors."

But George's book, coming out in 1885, was timely and useful, although as a profoundly philosophical work its permanent value of course far exceeds its value for the moment. In it he shows that freedom of exchange is not the isolated issue which politicians and publicists made it out to be, but is inextricably bound up with freedom of production. In fact, regarding it as an isolated issue, he showed that the protectionists must have pretty much the best of the argument. Ask an American free-trader of the "liberal" Sumner-Godkin type, who pointed to England as an example of free-trade practice, why it was that in free-trade England the labouring classes were worse off than in protectionist Germany—what could he answer? He could not answer. The only answer is that in England the principle of free trade was not carried out to its full logical length. George expounded the development of this principle; he was the first to do so. He proved that free exchange, the mere abolition of customs and custom-houses, could do nothing for the labouring classes, nothing for society-at-large, nor indeed could it do anything worth doing for anybody, unless it were correlated with freedom of production. He then went on to show, as Turgôt and Franklin had shown long before, that freedom of production could exist only where the land stood in open competition with industry in the labour-market; and in this way his exposition came straight around to the fundamental principles set forth in *Progress and Poverty*. Thus he showed that there is actually no such thing as a tariff-problem, any more than there is actually such a thing as a labour-problem; the only actual problem is the land-problem, and if that were solved, these two apparent problems would immediately disappear. *Protection or Free Trade* was a magnificent achievement in social philosophy, and one which, like *Progress and Poverty,* has never been successfully impugned.

IV

Ever since 1879, George had in the back of his mind the idea of a work which should coordinate and cover the whole science of political economy. At first he thought of writing a simple primer. Latterly, in the intervals of dabbling at *Protection or Free Trade,* he considered taking Adam Smith's *Wealth of Nations,* synopsizing the parts irrelevant to "a clear understanding of Smith's economy," annotating it, and publishing it at a popular price. In this way, he said, "I think I could make an exceedingly useful volume, rendering Smith much more intelligible to the general reader, and pointing out where he goes astray and all his successors have followed him." But later still, with his philosophical instinct once more sharp-set by his labours on *Protection or Free Trade,* the idea which he had "long contemplated" came to the fore. At this time, however, an interruption occurred which was in every way lamentable; and to the last degree lamentable because it was fatal to any further philosophical enterprise, and in its after-effects it was also fatal to him. A municipal election in New York City came on in 1886. Organized labour decided to go into the campaign with a ticket of its own, and pitched upon George as the likeliest vote-getter in sight, to be their candidate for the mayoralty.

It is a sordid story; sordid and squalid. George was reluctant to accept. His philosophical instinct prompted him against it; he told the first committee which waited on him that he had important work ahead which he would not willingly put off. He thought that ended the matter; indeed, at first he took the offer as more or less a compliment, very agreeable, but not to be regarded too seriously. He was in error about this, and should have known it at the outset; he should have known that he was being taken on because the labourites had no one else who could come anywhere near him in ability to attract votes. They told him that they would practically disregard the rest of their ticket and concentrate all their efforts on electing him; which in itself should have opened his eyes to the facts of the situation, but apparently it did not.

Failing in his first plea, he questioned the offer on prudential grounds. He said that there had been a good deal of dissension, rivalry and squabbling in the unionist ranks when previous attempts were made to inject organized labour into politics. Yes, the committee told him, that was true, but everything was harmonious now, and all hands were looking to him as the only one who could give them the leadership they needed in their struggle to relieve the oppressed and succour the downtrodden. This had a good sound, but George still hesitated; he seemed to suspect that it might be a little overdrawn. He finally put it that if the unions would bring him a petition signed by thirty thousand *bona fide* voters, he would accept the nomination. They accordingly did so, and accordingly he accepted.

It is vain to wonder what good George could possibly have expected to accrue from his election to the mayoralty of New York; what he thought he could by the wildest, the most unpredictable peradventure possibly make out of such a position as that. He never made it clear just what his actual expectations were, or whether he had any. He said the one thing sure was that "if I go into the fight, the campaign will bring the land question into politics, and do more to popularize its discussion than years of writing would do." So much for the campaign, but if elected, what then? His one proposal was to take the tax off buildings and put it on the land, exclusive of improvements; and this he would have found wholly impracticable, as anyone who had the slightest knowledge of the city's affairs could have told him. Perhaps he might have saved himself from the unfortunate step of accepting the nomination, if it had not been for the urgings of the friends he consulted, who were the very last persons competent to advise him. They were devotés of his person, energumens in his cause, who saw in a possible election the chance to make the mayoralty a beacon from which to spread the Light. Wiser persons on both sides of the Atlantic laboured with George, imploring him not to stultify himself so miserably, but all to no purpose. In accepting the nomination he said, "I believe, and have long believed, that workingmen ought to go into politics. I believe, and have long believed, that through politics was the way, and the only way, by which anything real and permanent could be secured for labour." It was a profession of faith wrought out, not by the philosopher of human freedom who said "I am for man," but by the Duke of Argyll's "prophet of San Francisco." As far as the current public estimate of him was concerned, it put the seal of finality upon the character he had chosen to give himself. Thenceforth he was irrevocably committed to be known *semper, ubique et ab omnibus,* as no more than the political file-leader of a class, a labour-skate.

The campaign was filthy and scurrilous beyond expression. Before the nominations were made, George was approached by a seasoned emissary of Tammany Hall, named William M. Ivins, a municipal jobholder, and a man of considerable prominence in the city, who had some pretensions to character. He had a deal to propose, and was very frank about it, telling George some quite interesting things concerning the way elections were actually managed. George said he "insisted that I could not be elected mayor of New York, no matter how many people might vote for me. . . . He said I could not possibly be counted in." Ivins offered George a seat in Congress if he would decline the nomination to the mayoralty. Tammany and the County Democracy would take care of him; all he need do was to forget it. Under this arrangement, George said, "I should be at no expense whatever, but might go to

An Essay

Europe or anywhere I willed, and when I came back should receive a certificate of election to the House of Representatives."

This was a pretty liberal offer. The mayoralty of New York was never a desirable place for a career-man; it was no stepping-stone to anything. On the other hand, assuming that George could have degenerated into the conventional type of politician, a break into Congress with the good-will of Tammany behind him—and Tammany never failed to do well by those who "went along"—meant an extremely good start for a man of George's ability. But why should Tammany be so keen to have George dodge the nomination? George put it to Ivins that if he could not be elected, as Ivins assured him he could not be, there seemed no reason *prima facie* why Tammany should make him this fine offer. Ivins said yes, it was true that he could not be elected, "but your running will raise hell." George replied that this was precisely what he wished it to do; and with that the conversation ended.

It is not quite true that the opposition to George was as largely engineered by "the forces of organized monopoly and greed" as his friends thought it was. There was that, of course; but he had against him also the considerable body of moderate and disinterested opinion which in America has always been apprehensive of what John Adams, Madison, Randolph, Gerry, Hamilton, foresaw as the "excesses," the "dangers," the "turbulence," of unchecked and unmodified mass-rule. Any candidate of a labour-unionist party would have encountered the same opposition. He also had the active ill-will of the Democratic organization in the city and county; and in a political way, he was by no means in the good graces of the local Roman hierarchy, for reasons which will appear later.

Nevertheless he made a good showing; he came near election, so near that one might reasonably suspect that he was counted out, as Ivins had warned him he would be. If indeed hell-raising were his intention, however, one must say that he succeeded admirably. Tammany was facing one of New York's recurrent spasms of "reform" which, if successful, meant that it would have to live on its fat for a couple of years or so. Hence Tammany wanted most of all to have things go on quietly, but George's campaign blew up those hopes with its broadsides against municipal corruption and graft. The "reform" candidate was elected—he was, by an odd coincidence, George's former employer, Abram S. Hewitt, a man of rather less than moderate ability, but a great deal of factitious dignity, one whom ribald persons nowadays would style as a stuffed shirt, and with whose candidacy Tammany would no doubt have had fairly easy rolling if it had not been for George.

The local Roman hierarchy also very much wanted things to go on quietly. The assumption that in this it was merely making itself the pliant tool of Tammany seems largely gratuitous. The Church had troubles of its own, precisely as it had had in Ireland, which were directly due to George. Some of its priests had gone in for George's economic system and had caught the infection of publicity from him; they were having too much to say about it. One priest in particular, Rev. Edward McGlynn, prominent in the diocese, rector of a large city parish, had for some time been hand-in-glove with George, and was now haranguing the multitude in favour of his election. The Church in New York felt the same displeasure at all this as the European authorities had felt in 1881 at similar activities on the part of the Irish bishop of Meath and some of his clergy. In both cases the

Church was in a hard position; it had to choose between ruffling great numbers of the faithful, and stretching discipline to the point of apparently countenancing a rather flagrant irregularity. In short, while neither the Church nor Tammany were in any actual fear of George, or anticipated any irreparable damage from his doings, they both alike regarded him as a most exasperating nuisance; which indeed, from their point of view, he was.

From the moment he accepted nomination to the mayoralty, George's prestige everywhere declined; nor does it appear that his defeat at all accelerated that decline. It was the nomination, not the election, which marked the high point of his career. At any time up to that point he could have recovered himself; the nomination was his last chance, the last red light of warning on the road which led to oblivion. By getting out of the arena of controversy, and resolutely staying out; by turning his back at once and forever on journalism, agitation, spellbinding, special pleading; by dissociating himself from those who were, as Spencer said, insuring the future ill-being of men while eagerly pursuing their present well-being; by firmly renouncing all thought of political action; by

An Essay

abandoning himself implicitly to the intimations of his philosophical instinct—by this he could, at any time up to the point of the nomination, have maintained himself in the historical position which rightfully was his to occupy.

V

With the passage of the crucial opportunity, the momentum of George's previous activities, like that of Macbeth's sins, marshalled him the way that he was going. He had eleven years to live, and inasmuch as his death, strictly speaking, came by accident, he might have had more; perhaps with care he might have had twice as many. From 1886 on, however, one might say his occupations and preoccupations were exclusively with politics and polemics. He sketched out his *Science of Political Economy* during this period, worked on it at intervals, but it always had to give way to the unceasing demands of politics and polemics, and was left incomplete.

In 1887, the year after his defeat for the mayoralty, he established his weekly paper, the *Standard,* devoted wholly to polemics and propaganda. He also led in organizing a third propagandist body essentially like the two which had earlier fallen by the wayside and perished of inanition. This was called the Anti-Poverty Society. It had a longer and more vigorous life than its predecessors, flourishing for a year, then splitting on a matter of national politics, and going under. Its prosperity was largely adventitious. Dr. McGlynn, its president, had been excommunicated from the Roman Catholic Church as the culmination of a *cause célèbre* which stirred up an immense amount of interest throughout the country, and such of this interest as was favourable, as well as a good deal of it that was merely curious, redounded to the benefit of the Anti-Poverty Society. Dr. McGlynn had a large personal following among his former parishioners as well, and with these as a sort of nucleus, he was able to run the local membership far up into the thousands.

In the same year George again ran for office as a labour-candidate, this time for a state office —secretary of state. Again he was reluctant, for prudential reasons. He thought that having been so lately unsuccessful in the city, the party would come off poorly in the state; but once more he consulted the wrong kind of friends, and once more he yielded to their bad advice. He made a brisk campaign, with Dr. McGlynn and other able speakers stumping the state for him, but his vote was inconsiderable; in New York City he polled but little more than half as many votes as he had got in the mayoralty election the year before.

All that the campaign did for him was to invigorate old enmities and create new ones; to confirm old misunderstandings and set up new ones; to chill off old friendships, and set no new ones alight; to blow the United Labour movement to pieces, and leave himself politically in the air. Even his staunch old friend and supporter, Patrick Ford, editor of the *Irish World,* broke with him and took the side of the Roman hierarchy in condemning the new Labour Party. George fell foul once more, as he had done in England, of the socialists who had tried to capitalize on the labour movement. Tammany gleefully put the harpoon in him on every possible occasion. His acquiescence in the shocking miscarriage of justice which hanged the Chicago anarchists, Spies, Parsons, Engel and Fischer, accused of complicity in the murder of certain policemen in 1885, alienated great numbers of people; and neither his attitude towards anarchism nor his attitude towards socialism conciliated a single one of those who regarded his own social doctrine as substantially on the same footing with either the one or the other.

Ten years later, in 1897, he entered another campaign at the head of an improvised new party, as an independent candidate for the mayoralty of New York; the party-title was the "Jeffersonian Party." The decade 1887-97 was one of the most extraordinary periods in all the history of America's fantastic civilization; even the period 1929-39 can do but little more than match its bizarre eccentricities. No one can describe that period; when the philosophical historian engages himself with it fifty years hence, he will think—and with reason—that he has come upon a nation of Bedlamites. Every imbecile socio-politico-economic nostrum that inspired idiocy could devise was trotted out and put on dress-parade for the immediate salvation of mankind. Free silver; the initiative, referendum and recall; farmer-labourism, votes-for-women, popular election of senators, the Wisconsin Idea, populism, prohibition, the Square Deal, direct primaries, Coxey and his army, Carry Nation and her hatchet, Coin Harvey and his primer—the list is without end.

This incredible irruption of frantic fatuity

had serious permanent effects upon the status of George and his doctrines. When it had spent itself and subsided, he was left as merely one more nostrum-pedlar among the many. His "Jeffersonian" campaign for the mayoralty marked him as merely one more visionary job-seeker, one with the Bryans and La Follettes of the century's turn. The tragic circumstances of George's death four days before the election gave rise everywhere to a most impressive demonstration of popular respect and sympathy, but as only for another good man gone wrong with the best of motives and the purest of intentions; motives and intentions, indeed, which had never been questioned—in this respect the popular estimate of George has always been, and still is, singularly correct. Circumstances being what they were, however, it was impossible to expect that even those—especially those—whom a disinterested examination of his philosophy would most have profited, should pick him out and disengage him from the welter of politico-economic insanity which raged around him.

Another damaging effect of circumstances was that a good deal of society's "lunatic fringe" which the period had released and made articulate, fastened on George's doctrine and perverted it with various adulterations. They associated it with other matters which interested them—matters ranging all the way from proportional representation to dietetics and promiscuous love-making—and viewed this association as natural and logical. Such as these had no power of discrimination, no power of establishing in their own minds the intrinsic relative importance of things; to them one nostrum was as weighty as another, if it but struck their disordered fancy to adopt it. After George's death, an increasing number of these pervaded what was known as the "single-tax movement," and did their full share to discredit it in the eyes of those who were uninformed about George's actual proposals, as well as those who had doubts of them on other grounds. An idea, like an individual, is largely judged by the company it keeps; and it was no recommendation of George's philosophy to hear it advocated by a professing single-taxer who was also a Bahaite, an interpreter of dreams and visions, a free-silverite, and who had theories concerning a nut-diet and the mystical number seven.

On a little higher plane were some who sophisticated George's fiscal proposals by dilution, some also by whittling down his policy of "Thorough." They became double-taxers in theory, or triple-taxers; they entertained various theoretical notions of compensation to landlords; some saw no inconsistency in swallowing a mild dose of protectionism. Very few would stand up to the doctrine of "Thorough"—the doctrine calling for the abolition of all taxes, and the substitution of a straight uncompensated confiscation of economic rent at full market-valuation and at one hundred cents in the dollar. But the final bad effect of a decade of utter intellectual dishevelment was to put the ethical side of George's philosophy quite completely aside and out of sight. Thenceforth, rather than as the proponent of human freedom, contemplating men as "endowed by their Creator with certain unalienable rights," he appeared only as the proponent of a new economic system. He who regarded his fiscal scheme as no more than a means to an ethical end—an indispensable means, indeed, but only a means nevertheless—thenceforth appeared as the proponent of his fiscal scheme as an end-in-itself; and this is the best that is made of him today, save by a very few.

8

THE late F. P. Dunne, speaking in the character of Mr. Dooley, remarked that "th' enthusiasm iv this counthry, Hinnissy, always makes me think iv a bonfire on an ice-floe. It burns bright so long as ye feed it, an' it looks good, but it don't take hold, somehow, on th' ice." The tremendous pother about "social reform" ran its customary short course and petered out, notwithstanding great effort by its energumens to keep it up. With this general decline of enthusiasm, interest in George's writings declined. His attack on Herbert Spencer, written in 1892, was comparatively little heeded. His weekly paper, the *Standard,* lost circulation steadily after the furore over the McGlynn case had subsided, and expired in 1892. George's unjustifiable utterances in defence of Dr. McGlynn put the *Standard* in the position of attacking the Church, and thereby greatly lessened its influence. While Dr. McGlynn was no doubt quite within his rights, and while the local authorities manifestly disregarded his rights in their treatment of him, there still seems something to be said on the local hierarchy's side. The case was mismanaged all round; it should have been managed not only with justice, but with the appearance of justice, for it was one of those matters where the appearance of justice is quite as important as justice itself. This necessary provision was overlooked by everyone concerned, and by none more consistently than by the editor of the *Standard*.

The archbishop of New York and his vicar-general were unfortunately not the kind of men to have such a matter in hand. Both exceeded their authority by misrepresenting the Church's doctrinal position. It would have been one thing to discipline Dr. McGlynn for public conduct unbecoming his profession; but it was quite another thing to discipline him for infidelity to doctrine. The one could have been done with justice, whether or not it was advisable to do it under the circumstances. The other could not have been done with justice under any circumstances. Both the archbishop and the vicar-general maintained that Dr. McGlynn was advocating principles and theories which were contrary to the teachings of the

Church, and this was simply not true. Five years later the Georgian scheme of land-value taxation which Dr. McGlynn advocated was overhauled by a committee of Roman theologians who found nothing in it contrary to the Church's teachings, and Dr. McGlynn was reinstated.

The unfortunate thing about George's part in the affair was that he acted as he did again in his attack on Herbert Spencer. He went behind the returns; he imputed motives without any evidence sufficient to sustain him. Surely it would be a serious thing—a very serious thing—to assume that Archbishop Corrigan and his vicar-general were not acting in good faith. A charge of ignorance was competent in the premises, as the outcome proved; a charge of hastiness, irritability, bad statesmanship, martinetism, culpable failure to examine the ground of action—this also was perfectly competent and could in all justice be made to stick. But a charge of deliberate bad faith was another matter; yet George wrote:

What Dr. McGlynn is punished for is for taking the side of the workingmen against the system of injustice and spoliation and the rotten rings which

An Essay

have made the government in New York a byword of corruption. . . . His sin is in taking a side in politics which was opposed to the rings that had the support of the Catholic hierarchy.

This was going behind the returns at a great rate; not only was it a charge of bad faith, but it was also an imputation of the next thing to criminal connivance. No wonder that George's hold on the public was weakening, or that on all sides he was accused of "attacking the Catholic Church"; no wonder that the more judicious among his intimates shook their heads sadly as they saw public sentiment, which seldom errs on the side of charity in matters of this kind, turning more and more to his disadvantage.

In May, 1891, after the local furore over Dr. McGlynn had died out, His Holiness Leo XIII issued the notable encyclical *Rerum novarum,* on the condition of labour. George, with his mind at once forced back on his brush with the diocesan authorities in New York, took the encyclical as aimed directly at his economic doctrines. Under ordinary circumstances it would seem to need a deal of self-consciousness to entertain this notion, for on the face of it the letter certainly suggests no such interpretation.

On a fair reading today, one would certainly say it was unlimbered against nothing but the collectivism which George detested quite as cordially as the Holy Father did. Whatever other intention could be strained out of it must be got at through those familiar methods of "judicial interpretation" whereby, as a contemporary of Bishop Butler said, anything can be made to mean anything.

Nor is it at all likely *a priori* that His Holiness would have any erroneous doctrine in mind but the socialism which he repeatedly arraigns by name. Still less likely is it that with his sources of information what they were, he would have fallen into the vulgar error of using socialism as a generic term to cover anything to which it was inapplicable, let alone something diametrically its opposite. Papa Pecci, servant of the servants of God, was a very great man; great as a saint, great as a scholar, theologian, philosopher, man of letters. In statesmanship, he was far and away the greatest of the century's four great creative minds. To find his equal, one must scan very closely the whole long list of those who have occupied the chair of St. Peter, and then one is not sure. Hence when he spoke, it is highly probable that he quite knew what he was talking about and quite meant what he said, no more, no less.

Moreover, it hardly appears that the case of Dr. McGlynn excited anywhere near as much commotion and searching of heart in Rome as it did in New York. When Cardinal Gibbons brought the matter up at Rome in 1887, both the Holy Father and the cardinal-prefect of the Propaganda told him that so far from condemning Dr. McGlynn or his teachings, they had passed no judgment whatever on the case. In the view of the Vatican it was apparently a local issue. Five years later, when Dr. McGlynn went to Rome immediately after his reinstatement, the Holy Father asked him whether he taught against private property. Dr. McGlynn said no, he never had; he had always been staunch for private property. "I thought so," said Papa Pecci, and gave him his blessing; and that seemed to be all there was to that.

Curiously, however, George wrote a correspondent that "for my part, I regard the encyclical letter as aimed at us, and at us alone, almost." He thought he "ought to write something about it," with the old inveterate propagandist purpose; such a reply "might give an opportunity of explaining our principles to many people who know little or nothing about them." Accordingly he devoted the whole summer of 1891 to this project, publishing the result in the form of an open letter to His Holiness, four months after the publication of the encyclical. It was brought out in New York and London, and at Rome in an Italian version. A handsome copy was put in the Pope's hands, and George thought the circumstances of Dr. McGlynn's reinstatement a year afterward indicated that the Pope had read it, which seems unlikely. Probably it was looked over by someone in authority who no doubt thought it was very fine, very good, but since it did not bear particularly on anything His Holiness had said, there was no use in its going further. At any rate, whether or not anybody in the Vatican ever read it, Leo XIII made no acknowledgment of the gift at any time.

He could hardly have done so. The only acknowledgment he could have made was in the way of a fatherly hint that George should not cry before he was hurt; and that obviously would be impracticable. It is clear that the Vatican never regarded George's views as anything but "free doctrine." The encyclical bore down heavily on land-nationalization, but it

An Essay

was the socialists, not George, who advocated that; George was against it, all along—he was for nationalizing the economic rent of land, which is another matter entirely, and collides with nothing that the Pope had to say. Private monopoly of land is one thing; the Pope was for it, and so was George. Private monopoly of the economic rent of land is quite another thing; George was against it, and the Pope said nothing about it. Of course one may always assign any amount of importance to whatever implications one chooses to construe out of silence; but in doing that one should be sure that circumstances make one's constructions at least plausible.

When George wrote His Holiness that "your encyclical will be seen by those who carefully analyze it to be directed, not against socialism, which in moderate form you favour, but against what we in the United States call the single tax"—he was going behind the returns most unwarrantably. He was proceeding by pure arbitrary inference, with no ground of demonstrable fact to go on. Moreover, the gravamen of the statement was distinctly offensive, as will be perceived at once; it amounted to saying that the Holy Father either ignorantly or deliberately misdirected the incidence of his censure; and this, to say the least of it, was an extremely serious assumption.

The letter to the Pope, like the attack on Herbert Spencer, which George published in the following year, 1892, under the title, *A Perplexed Philosopher,* produced little effect. Neither work provoked anything like the discussion which George expected; few were interested in them, fewer were enlightened by them. The country was tapering off from its delirious debauch on nostrums of one kind and another, and was getting into the mood of Col. Asa Bird Gardiner's famous saying, "To hell with reform!" It was preparing the path for Hanna and the full dinner-pail in 1896, for McKinley and imperialism in 1897, for Roosevelt and the policies of "practical men," for dollar-diplomacy and a long run of diligent imperialist buccaneering. George and his remaining friends were fish out of water, washed up on the bank and left there, high and dry.

George had misgivings about his last two productions, the letter to the Pope, and the broadside against Spencer. He was doubtful about their being worth the time taken away from his work on political economy. After they

An Essay

were written, he thought more than once that his labour on them was largely wasted and that the time spent on them was misspent. It is interesting to observe here the persistence of vitality in a true instinct so long repressed and suffocated. In 1891, speaking of his projected work on the science of political economy, he wrote a friend that he had long thought "perhaps it would be useful if I could put the ideas embodied in *Progress and Poverty* in the setting of a complete economic treatise, and without controversy." *Without controversy*—there spoke the sound philosophical instinct, with what was virtually its dying breath, and its last words were those which prompted doubt about the worthwhileness of his two controversial essays.

Seven years were none too many for such a task as his proposed work on political economy, and in all probability George might have had more than seven. If he had devoted even seven years to that work, assuming that he was to have but seven, what a work it might, nay, certainly would, have been! For the first time in his life, moreover, he could have carried on a piece of sustained work undisturbed by the fear of want. He had been ill and broken by his incessant labours, and two rich friends now took him in hand, insisting that he drop the *Standard* and enjoy an independent existence in reasonable comfort. George might well have taken this occurrence as an "intimation of the dæmon" that the work he contemplated was the one which he was called upon to do. But the Pope's encyclical intervened, Spencer's recantation intervened, a free-trade campaign in Congress intervened, forlorn local single-tax campaigns here and there intervened, all devouring his time and addling his attention—the habit of years was too strong to be broken, however much he might have wished to break it—and then came the hopeless and preposterous campaign for the mayoralty of New York in 1897, which led directly to his death.

II

A small compact host of disciples carried on the "single-tax movement" after George's death, with singular energy and devotion. Their efforts emphasized the fiscal features of his system, laying relatively little stress on the system's ethical aim. Since their policy was one of mass-conversion, this was reasonable, perhaps necessary; the masses could be best caught by an exposition of effect on the pocket-book, and once caught by that, they would be better disposed to consider the system's ethical features. Yet inevitably this tended to push those features more and more out of the popular view, and more and more to cause the system to be popularly regarded as of a purely economic character. George the philosopher of freedom, George the exponent of individualism as against Statism, George the very best friend the capitalist ever had, George the architect of a society based on voluntary coöperation rather than on enforced coöperation— this George, the truly great, the incomparable George, sank out of sight, leaving only George the economic innovator, the author of a new and untried method of laying taxes.

George's course of public conduct, ill-advised as one may think it was, unsound as its fundamental postulate may appear to be, was directed towards the ethical end contemplated by his philosophy, and that end alone. It never varied; in all his preoccupations with the means to that end there was never in his own mind an instant of confusion of them with the end. When a silly person told him that the single-tax is not a panacea, he replied that he was well aware it is not, "but freedom is; and the single-tax is the way to freedom." All his battles were fought to vindicate the natural rights of man as against those who would deny or over-ride them. In its eloquent attestation of this purpose, and of the ethical sanction which he invoked upon this purpose, his letter to the Pope has great permanent value. As an *apologia pro vita sua* its value even exceeds that of the section which ends *Progress and Poverty*. Probably no one can quite complete his understanding of George, or quite round out an appreciation of him, without a sympathetic reading and re-reading of this letter.

III

In their efforts to further the "single-tax movement," George's disciples have followed his methods; the methods of evangelizing, of organizing, of seeking political action. Judged in relation to the amount of time, energy and money spent on these methods, their success is not impressive; so little impressive, in fact, as to suggest their utter incompetence. A reading of Mr. Geiger's excellent book shows how hard one is put to it to discern the survival of any substantial influence which the continuators of George's teachings may have exerted; and a re-

An Essay

view of George's career, such as has been attempted in this present essay, seems appropriate in order to show, among other things, why this influence is so slight.

The methods of George's disciples were based on the same postulate which he accepted concerning the moral and intellectual capacities of mankind. If that postulate be sound, then obviously George was right in his choice of methods, and the results might be expected to show, at least measurably, that he was right. Similarly, to take the most conspicuous example by way of comparison, if this eighteenth-century postulate of Condorcet and Rousseau be sound, the practice of even the pseudo-republicanism in vogue for a century and a half should be measurably attesting its soundness; it should at least be demonstrating that a closer approach to true republicanism is expedient and desirable. So should the practice of free public education; so should all the collective practices whose institution is referable to that postulate. On the other hand, if no such attestation appears in any instance, if results are negative or positively unfavourable, the postulate is in doubt. There is no way of judging save by the results of practical experimentation, because the postulate is purely conjectural. One can not keep too constantly in mind the fact that this was a sheer speculation on the part of its projectors in the eighteenth century; an interesting speculation, highly flattering to the masses of mankind and therefore most acceptable, but nevertheless a sheer speculation.

It met no serious challenge in the nineteenth century, and up to very lately it has met none in the twentieth. Man's incapacities were generally ascribed to conditions, as George ascribed them; they were environmental in origin, not constitutional. A larval capacity was there, and one-or-another shift of external stimulus would bring it into play—more experience, more education, more responsibility, more-this, more-that. As the masses of mankind increasingly assumed control of civilization's immediate destinies, however, doubts began to be expressed about the correctness of this view, and it became apparent that the fundamental postulate supporting this view would stand re-examination.

Naturally so, because there can now be no question that the masses' assumption of control has issued in a prompt and swift degeneration throughout the world's whole social order. In the United States, for example, the progressive mass-control of public affairs has brought to pass precisely the state of things which George forecast in *Progress and Poverty,* in the chapter entitled, "How Modern Civilization May Decline"—a chapter which will interest anyone as a model of accurate prediction, whatever may be thought about the premises on which the prediction is based. The degree to which distinctively human qualities have degenerated under the sanction of a completely universal suffrage—under the consent that number should count for everything, and all other qualifications, or their absence, should count for nothing—is in itself sufficiently remarkable and startling to suggest a revision of eighteenth-century theory concerning the nature of man. A clear consciousness of this pervades modern critical thought as expressed in the admirable work of Dr. Carrel, of Spengler, Ortega y Gasset and others; and the undercurrent of uneasy doubt and questioning is perceptible almost wherever one may choose to feel for it.

It seems then that henceforth any review of George's career must take into account the question whether the general incapacity for acceptance of his philosophy, or of any philosophy, is circumstantial and temporary, or constitutional and permanent. Were the eighteenth-century philosophers right or wrong? The ethical scheme of Philadelphian society in the 'thirties—was its fundamental postulate of human perfectibility sound or unsound? Were the Rev. Josiah Jupp and Mr. Creakle, whatever their divagations, proceeding on the strength of a sound fundamental principle, or on the weakness of an unsound one? Was Herbert Spencer's optimism, based on the assumption of indefinite time, actually any more tenable than George's optimism which disallowed and disregarded that assumption?

Such questions as these, then, would appear to be henceforth most appropriate for our revisions of history and biography to entertain. Some vague instinctive sense of this may perhaps even now be evident in the attitude of George's disciples of the second generation who have abandoned the idea of proselytizing-at-large. Perhaps, on the other hand, they have merely made the salutary observation that the world's great philosophers never contemplated a mass-acceptance of themselves or their doctrines, but only their acceptance by an élite. At all events, they are apparently bringing their efforts in behalf of George's philosophy into line with this expectation, and therein they act wisely. "He that hath ears *to hear*," said the *Santissimo Salvatore*, "let him hear." Everyone has ears; Murdstone, Quinion, the Akka, the bushman, the African pigmy, all have ears, mostly very acute ears; but relatively few have ears *to hear*.

It is perhaps unnecessary to point out, however, that the entertainment of these questions has, and can have, no bearing whatever on the validity of George's philosophy, but only on the conditions of its acceptance. After surviving twenty years of controversy unharmed, untouched, it seems improbable that his philosophy will ever need review, reappraisal or even restatement. As it now stands it will apparently forever continue to fulfil perfectly the functions of a social philosophy as they are described by Spencer. It will continue to locate and identify the ideal which is needful for right guidance, however far in advance of practicability; considerations of practicability simply do not appear, they are not in its purview. It will continue to establish true conceptions of better and worse in social organizations; to look steadily beyond the exigencies of the moment; to differentiate sharply between the proximately-best and the ultimately-best; and to reprehend those who habitually identify the proximately-best with the ultimately-best, thus "insuring the future ill-being of men while eagerly pursuing their present well-being."

Nor is it at all implied that if the average of mankind is permanently incapable of accepting a philosophy, it is incapable of accepting the fruits of a philosophy, for even the dullest and most self-willed of domesticated animals are capable of that. Hence whether the foregoing questions be settled in one way or another, the settlement offers no insurmountable bar to a practical realization of George's philosophy; it merely helps towards an intelligent determination of the conditions necessary for realizing it. It is clear now, for example, that this realization is to all appearances impracticable under a quasi-republican organization of society, and the closer the approach to true republicanism, the worse the outlook. This, however, does not make against its practicability under some other scheme of social organization; indeed, it makes some useful suggestions about the form or mode which a scheme most favourable to an implantation of George's philosophy might assume. Therefore in this as in all other respects, the consideration of these questions is quite as encouraging as it is profitable.

IV

Finally we may remind ourselves that any reappraisal of George, whenever made, must end as it must begin, in reverent regard for the one quality which most conspicuously sets him off against the background of the society he lived in—the quality of simple human goodness. He was one of the greatest of philosophers, and the spontaneous concurring voice of all his contemporaries acclaimed him as one of the best of men. Erasmus made it a mark of true Christians that they should be so blameless as to force infidels to speak well of them, and this George was. In the midst of an evil and perverse generation he walked worthily; in a welter of the worst passions and the meanest prejudices he remained innocent, sincere, steadfast. He is with Marcus Aurelius as "one of those consoling and hope-inspiring marks which stand forever to remind our weak and easily-discouraged race how high human goodness and perseverance have once been carried, and may be carried again." In time to come, the élite of mankind shall say, "It was a society which did only what was right in its own eyes. Its works and ways bore only the mark of Rimmon upon them; the people took up the tabernacle of Moloch and Chiun, their images; they followed the star of their god Remphan. Yet there were some who were incorruptible, who walked not after strange gods; their eye was single; and one of them was called Henry George."